WALKING ROUND THE LAKES

THE WALK

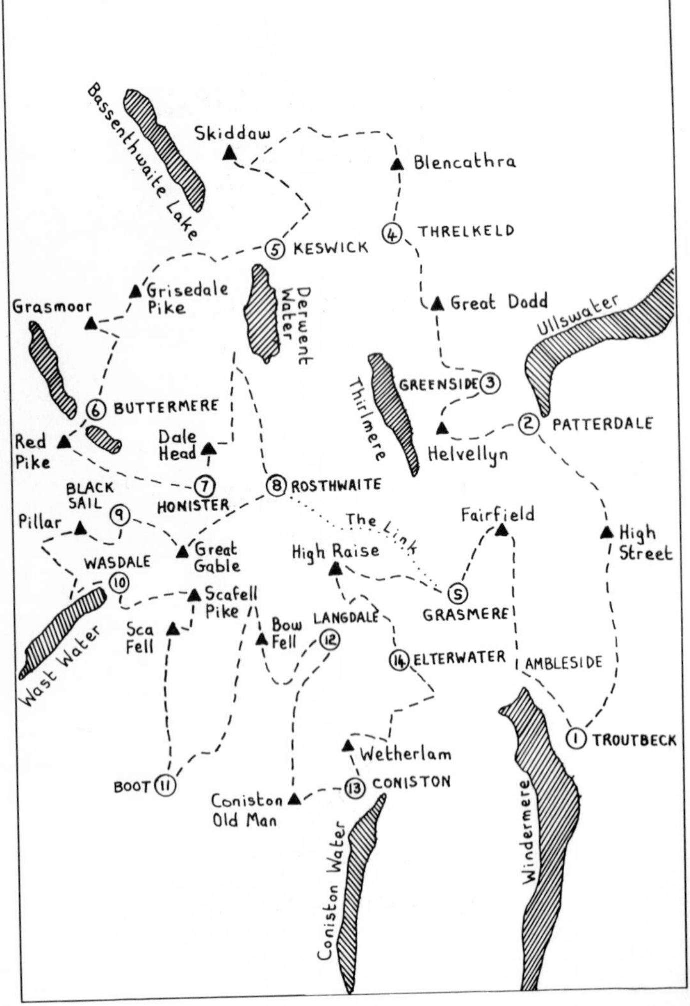

Bassenthwaite Lake
Skiddaw
Blencathra
THRELKELD
KESWICK
Grisedale Pike
Grasmoor
Derwent Water
Great Dodd
Ullswater
Thirlmere
GREENSIDE
BUTTERMERE
PATTERDALE
Helvellyn
Red Pike
Dale Head
ROSTHWAITE
HONISTER
BLACK SAIL
Pillar
The Link
Fairfield
High Street
Great Gable
High Raise
WASDALE
GRASMERE
Scafell Pike
Sca Fell
Bow Fell
LANGDALE
ELTERWATER
AMBLESIDE
Wast Water
Wetherlam
TROUTBECK
BOOT
CONISTON
Coniston Old Man
Coniston Water
Windermere

WALKING ROUND THE LAKES

by

John and Anne Nuttall

Maps and drawings by
John Nuttall

CICERONE PRESS
MILNTHORPE, CUMBRIA

ISBN 1 85284 099 4

Front Cover: The head of Wast Water
Back Cover: Striding Edge

CONTENTS

KEY

road	
track	
path	
river	
stream	
footbridge	FB
Church	▪ Ch
Youth Hostel	▪ YH
Start (each day)	(S)
End day	(6)

fence

wall

fences and walls beside tracks omitted for clarity

wood

contours at 50m
- 300 -
- 350 -
- 400 -

cliffs and steep rocks

scree

2000ft summit ▲ 768 height in metres

other cairns △

	on path	on track	on road
Low Route	....	.=.=.=	
High Route	- - - -	====	

Route - no path — . — . —

Route at edge of map marked in margin thus

High Route from previous page (H)

Low Route   "   "   "   (L)

To Map number ➤ 9·2

SCALE 2½" = 1 mile

INTRODUCTION

In the late sunshine of an autumn afternoon we walked down from Helvellyn at the end of one of the most enjoyable times ever on the Lake District fells. For five days we had walked among the mountains, visiting in turn the Scafells, Skiddaw and Helvellyn and each night we had set up our mountain tent hidden high and wild in the fells. Some nights we had lain listening to the rain and in the morning woken to sparkling ice-crystalled surroundings. On other days the clouds parted and brief shafts of sunlight picked out golden summits amid the surrounding black fells. On the Scafells the mist was down and, making an early start from Sprinkling Tarn, we were away before seven walking alone over the tops in a silent grey world. Skiddaw was equally grey as in steady rain we crossed the summit to camp in a sheepfold amid the deserted fells Back o'Skiddaw, but on Helvellyn the sun shone and as we descended to Grisedale Tarn we were already planning our next expedition.

To take five days over the Lake District three-thousanders may seem rather sluggish, but it wasn't just that we walked slowly, there was simply so much to see on the way. Lakes, tarns, the flowers, the rocks, the view from each top, none of this could be hurried. There was only one way the walk could be improved and that was to take even longer, so while fell runners strive to fit more and more fells into the day, we decided to fit more and more days into the fells. It was fell running, though, that suggested our next objective and the route we chose was one which had been devised nearly sixty years ago: 'The Bob Graham Round'.

Bob Graham was a Keswick guest house owner with a passion for fell running and an ambition to beat the record held by Eustace Thomas, a Manchester businessman who had climbed the greatest number of Lake District fells in the space of 24 hours. His first attempt in 1931 was abandoned due to bad weather and problems with route finding, but the following year, on June 13, a new record was achieved. For the next twenty-eight years this record remained unbroken, a feat which included a total of forty-two peaks and covered 72 miles with 27,000 feet of ascent. Although the record has been broken several times since, the repeat of the original round has become a tradition among athletes who have formed a club, the Bob Graham Club, for people completing the round within 24 hours.

No, we didn't run it. By taking our time and enjoying the views, we set a new kind of record. Eight days for the Bob Graham Round can seldom have been equalled and as we walked into Keswick, where tradition requires that you must touch the Moot Hall to finish, we felt as pleased as any exhausted runner.

The trouble with the Bob Graham Round is that it leaves out so much. The Coniston fells are missed entirely, as are the Kentmere and the Far

Eastern fells and no sooner have you struggled to the top of Fairfield than an about-turn is made back down to Grisedale Tarn. To make it a proper walk many more fells are needed and more fells means a longer walk.

Devising a route gave us a great deal of enjoyment with the maps spread out on the lounge floor as we planned days which linked the fells together into one continuous walk. Every night would be spent in a new place, but unlike most other long distance walks this one would be circular and would finish in the place from which it started.

We walked every section twice, some in the hazy heat of summer, some in the middle of winter, in the spring with the flowers and in the autumn with the fall of the leaves. Much of the time we camped and with settled weather our tent was pitched on many of the mountain summits under starlit skies. These wild camps have given us some of the best memories: lying in our tent on the summit of High Raise just before going to sleep, looking out on the orange afterglow of the sunset and the blue-grey silhouettes of Great Gable and the Scafells; reaching the deserted summit of Wetherlam early in the morning on a clean, clear sunny day in spring, when all the fells, still with the russet colours of autumn, looked fresh and new; coming down to the Tilberthwaite valley where the woods were bright with bluebells, celandines, red campion, wood anemonies and wood sorrel; a night spent on Scafell Pike and waking to a morning so still that we could hear the faint sounds of the valley awakening to another day drifting up; and, perhaps the best of all, when we climbed one December morning from a grey Braithwaite valley through the cloud into a world of brilliant white above the clouds.

Yet even after a night of heavy and continuous rain when we discovered the tent was in the centre of a lake, or days when ice and snow covered the fells and nothing could be seen in the grey mist covering the tops, days when we struggled bent double against the wind, or days when yet again it rained from morning to evening and then again all night, we loved the fells.

In the end the route was a compromise. Several delightful ways were chosen and then discarded when they ended the day miles from suitable lodgings for the night. Many summits which we would have liked to include were regretfully omitted and there was always the temptation to make every day that little bit longer, yet no-one, even after a lifetime spent among these hills, claims to know everything about them and a fortnight is barely sufficient to provide an aperitif. But if at the end of the walk you want to come back, perhaps next time to spend longer in one spot, if perhaps like us you have fallen in love with the fells, then we shall have passed on some of the magic which it has provided for us.

NOTES

The Lake District is not much more than 30 miles across and some 40 miles from north to south. It is quite possible to walk right across it in a couple of days. But what a waste! There is more loveliness packed into its 866 square miles than anywhere else in Great Britain and the best way to get to know it is to go for a walk.

Walking Round the Lakes is a circular walk of fifteen days which encompasses all the major summits in the Lake District. Each of the fourteen nights is spent in a different place and while the High Level Route traverses the mountain tops, an alternative Low Level Route is described for each day to cater for bad weather. The route in total covers 145 miles with around 50,000 feet of ascent though the Low Level alternatives are shorter and with less ascent.

If fifteen days is more than can be spared at one time the final section of the book describes The Link which splits the walk into two separate weeks.

Accommodation

At the end of each day's walk there is a choice of places to stay. The Lake District is well supplied with youth hostels, bed and breakfast establishments, pubs and hotels, but as it gets very busy in the season it is advisable to book in advance. All except three of the fourteen nights have a convenient youth hostel and there is always more luxurious accommodation available. Campers are well catered for as there is a nearby campsite each night, except for Grasmere at the start of the walk which is above such things.

No attempt has been made to give detailed accommodation lists as these become rapidly out of date, but at the end of the book there is a general information table which we hope will prove helpful when planning the tour.

The Start

The tour starts in Grasmere, but as it is circular it is possible to begin anywhere you like as after fifteen days you will arrive back at the same place! Grasmere is a conveniently central spot, easily accessible by bus from either Keswick or Windermere and the railway station. There are two large car parks where, at the time of writing, cars can be left for a long stay. The local information centres and the police will also give advice as to where to leave vehicles. It is not a good idea to just abandon your car by the side of the road or you may find the mountain rescue has been out searching for you when you return.

Route Choice

The walk has been planned so that the average fell walker can see as much as possible of the Lake District hills in fifteen days of not too strenuous walking over the fell tops.

A route summary is given at the beginning of each day listing the distance and the height to be climbed, a brief outline of the route and an indication of the nature of the terrain. Distances are measured each day mostly from the youth hostels though where there is no hostel a central point is chosen instead.

Lake District terrain varies from the easy grass slopes of the north-western fells to the very rough rocks and boulders of Scafell Pike, so the time taken each day is not just a matter of distance and ascent. People vary too, and while one group will find the days on the short side, others will find them plenty long enough, but all can be accomplished by an average walker in a day without rushing things. It is also possible, by using the alternative stopping places listed in the table at the end of the book, to shorten or lengthen the days to suit both potterers and supermen. Though most of the route is on paths, one or two sections require simple pathless navigation using a compass.

Lake District weather is not always kind, so each day an alternative and easier Low Route is given. This is less strenuous and avoids the high ridges though on some days it climbs over a high pass in order to cross into the next valley.

Maps

Most people like to find north at the top of the map, so that is the way they have all been drawn. There is an overall plan of the route, while maps A E show the High and Low Route choice over several days. The detailed maps for each day, which are included with the text, are at a scale of 1:25,000. To complement the walk the OS Lake District Tourist Map is useful for identifying the views, giving a general picture of the countryside and for linking the days together as a whole, while for anyone exploring off the route there is nothing to beat the four Outdoor Leisure Maps of the English Lakes which cover the whole walk.

Weather

The walk can be done at any time of the year, each season having its own charm. In winter the days are short and snow and ice can turn the fells into a serious mountaineering challenge necessitating the use of ice axes and crampons. Winter conditions may persist as late as Easter, especially on the eastern ridges of Helvellyn, so care must be taken then. Spring and autumn are supposedly the driest times in the Lakes but the long days of summer have the advantage, especially if you are camping, of the extra daylight when it gets dark 45 minutes later than it does in London.

A daily weather forecast of the fell top conditions is available on Windermere 05394 45151.

Equipment

It does rain sometimes in the Lake District, so even in the height of summer be prepared for bad weather. Even if you plan to go the whole way on the Low Route boots are a necessity, as are a waterproof top and trousers, hat and gloves even in midsummer, and a whistle and compass.

The Link

While the complete Tour of the Lakes takes fifteen days, it can be divided into two separate weeks, the first covering the eastern and northern fells, and the second the western and southern fells. The Link Route is the connection which returns you to Grasmere at the end of the first week. The walk may be resumed another time by reversing The Link.

As each of the two halves also gives a circular walk the start can be varied to suit the walker.

Although the Link is described as starting from Rosthwaite giving nine days of walking, it is just as easy to return from Honister, making eight days in all, by first walking down the Honister Pass. This adds on a couple of extra miles, but it is all downhill.

Bridge House, Ambleside

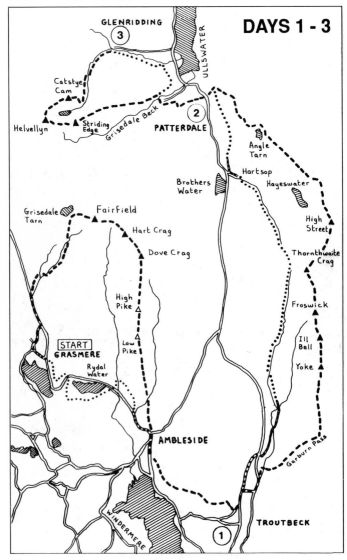

GLENRIDDING
3

ULLSWATER

DAYS 1 - 3

Catstye Cam

Helvellyn
Striding Edge
Grisedale Beck

2

PATTERDALE

Angle Tarn

Hartsop
Hayeswater

Brothers Water

High Street

Grisedale Tarn
Fairfield

Hart Crag

Dove Crag

Thornthwaite Crag

High Pike

Froswick

Low Pike

START
GRASMERE

Rydal Water

Ill Bell

Yoke

AMBLESIDE

Garburn Pass

WINDERMERE

TROUTBECK

1

Fairfield and Grisedale Tarn

DAY 1 GRASMERE TO TROUTBECK

HIGH LEVEL ROUTE	Distance 12½ miles	Ascent 3,700ft
LOW LEVEL ROUTE	Distance 8 miles	Ascent 1,200ft

ROUTE SUMMARY

High Level Route Climbing by way of the old packhorse track to Grisedale Tarn, the route continues up steep scree slopes to Fairfield, then traversing the tops of Hart Crag and Dove Crag the grassy ridge descends over High Pike and Low Pike into Ambleside. Here the Low Level Route is joined for the final section over Jenkin Crag to the scattered hamlet of Troutbeck. Apart from the Fairfield scree the paths are good throughout with only short sections of rough going.

Low Level Route After passing Dove Cottage, the lower slopes of Loughrigg Fell are crossed to visit a huge quarry cave. Descending to Rydal Water and Rydal, another stop on the Wordsworth Trail, a stroll through Rydal Park leads to Ambleside where the routes combine.

From the village of Rydal, midway between Grasmere and Ambleside, the valley of Rydal Beck cuts north into the hills. On either side fine high ridges form a horseshoe enfolding the valley and at the head is Fairfield, one of the giants of the Eastern Fells. The hills of the western arm, Nab Scar, Heron Pike and Great Rigg, rise in a series of mainly grassy steps to the broad, flat, stony summit of Fairfield, while on the eastern side, overlooking Deepdale and Dovedale, are the much rockier Dove Crag and Hart Crag.

It is not, however, the individual summits that are the focus of attention as many who frequent these tops might be hard pressed to say without hesitation whether they were standing on Hart Crag or Dove Crag, but these fells are known collectively as the Fairfield Horseshoe, one of the most popular hill walks in the Lakes.

The Lake District abounds in semi-circular walks because of its topography, a series of ridges radiating from a central hub, and it was Wordsworth who, in his *Guide to the Lake District*, first likened this arrangement of the fells to the spokes of a wheel. Although it must be apocryphal, the tale is that one enthusiast commending his excellent book, enquired of the poet whether he had written anything else. This guide followed some fifty years after the first guide book to the Lakes by Thomas West, which was published in 1778. Wordsworth himself quotes West on the Vale of Grasmere where the tour begins

14

Not a single red tile, no flaring gentleman's house or garden-wall, breaks in upon the repose of this little unsuspected paradise; but all is peace, rusticity, and happy poverty, in its neatest and most becoming attire.

Starting from Grasmere it would be difficult to avoid Wordsworth. For nine years Dove Cottage, just off the A591 on the old road to Rydal, was his home. Here he came in 1799 with his devoted and adoring sister Dorothy. Here he stayed after his marriage to Mary Hutchinson in 1802 and although later he moved to Allan Bank and then up the road to Rydal, here he lies buried, in a simple grave in the little churchyard.

Dove Cottage

Dove Cottage is, despite the concentrated attention it receives from over 80,000 visitors every year, still charming, its little garden faithfully set out as it was when William paced its short terrace intent upon his composition. Our first visit to Dove Cottage was on our honeymoon and we had it to ourselves until we were joined in the kitchen by an earnest American lady who enquired eagerly if the soap in the sink was the poet's own soap. On our last visit a log fire burned brightly in the grate and while a thunderstorm raged outside we again had a solitary tour in the helpful and informative company of one of the guides, a philosophy graduate.

The cottage, which stands on the old turnpike road and was built in the seventeenth century, was originally the Dove and Olive Branch public house. In Wordsworth's day the outlook would have been much more open as the present main road by the lake was not built until 1823 and Grasmere could be seen. Samuel Taylor Coleridge, Scott and de Quincy all visited here and when the Wordsworths moved to Allan Bank, Dove Cottage was taken by de Quincy where he wrote *Confessions of an English Opium Eater.*

If at times the village overflows with the thousands on the Wordsworth Trail and the many more thousands who've come just because everyone else has, then perhaps one wishes that Wordsworth had lived somewhere else like Wigan or Wolverhampton. Nevertheless, if it wasn't for his determined and elitist defence of the Lake District we might well have a railway to Ambleside and widespread major development and have lost for ever a priceless treasure.

One of the principal guardians of the Lake District is, of course, the National Trust which, widely respected for its care of England's stately homes, has now turned its attention to repairing the eroded trackways of the Lakes. The results have been excellent, with good paths quickly blending into the hillside where only rivers of scree ran before. They are copying the old method of 'pitching' used on the ancient packhorse routes across the major passes of the Lake District. Large stones from the fellside or the beds of adjacent streams are set into the ground, fitting together like a jigsaw, and the gaps filled with gravel and soil. Large stones are used to hold the edges of the path and gutters are constructed to shed water. The packhorse route from Grasmere to Grisedale Tarn has recently been expertly repaired in this way. The National Trust has already spent hundreds of thousands of pounds rebuilding the worst of the eroded paths in the Lakes, but the work is slow as well as expensive, four people in one gang averaging just ten yards per day.

It was late evening as we climbed the newly laid stones of the old packhorse track to Grisedale Tarn. We had spent a pleasant evening at the Travellers' Rest. A good meal, a chat with a couple from Bangor University and we were gradually becoming sleepy in front of the open fire. It was time for bed, but bed was to be beside Grisedale Tarn nearly two thousand feet up and now it was cold, it was raining in a fitful sort of way and while we climbed, the cloud rolled down to meet us.

As the dark waters of the tarn came into view the wind rose, whipping the water into waves whose breaking white tops were the only things visible in the grey twilight. The far end of the tarn must surely be sheltered, but when we reached it the wind roared, shaking violently some small tents pitched on the shore. We turned back up the tarn to find protection in the lee of Seat Sandal as twilight gave way to night.

A few minutes later life was transformed. The tent was up. We were in our sleeping bags. The kettle was simmering on the stove and our home was lit by the friendly glow of our torches. It was a peaceful night. From time to time we woke to hear the rain on the tent and dozed off again, then suddenly, at about 3 am, a voice just outside the tent called "Chris!" and then again, a little further away "Chris!" It was a bad night to be on the Bob Graham Round.

The next morning was cold and grey, but dry, and soon we were climbing the steep scree slopes to Fairfield. Grisedale Tarn lay blackly below, a very different picture from when we once bathed there and climbed Fairfield after dinner in a thick heat haze. Then, no sooner had we reached the summit than a crash and rumble of thunder from towards Windermere sent us scurrying back down to learn the next day that a boat on the lake had been struck by lightning and burnt out.

A runner passed us near the top, dressed in shorts and a thin top. Even in waterproofs we were far from warm and as we reached the cairn we were surprised to find him jogging round looking expectantly towards Helvellyn. "They should be along any minute," he said, gesturing to the steep scree slopes of Dollywagon Pike. "It's the Bob Graham Relay Race." We sheltered behind the cairn and had some chocolate. He looked frozen. "I'm a marshal," he confided, "I'm sure they should be here soon." But the figures who appeared ten minutes later were not the runners, but scouts. "We left the tents at the tarn," they said. "Luckily only one of them blew down last night." "We were up here yesterday," they went on. "It was very interesting. It was the Bob Graham Relay." We looked round for the marshal, but he had gone.

ROUTE DESCRIPTION

HIGH LEVEL ROUTE
From Sam Read's bookshop beside the green in the centre of **Grasmere** the road leads out to the busy A591. After crossing the River Rothay fork left along Pye Lane and then left up the main road past the Travellers' Rest. At Mill Bridge the public bridleway to Patterdale turns right up a rough, stony track and this old packhorse way climbs gently above the bracken-covered slopes of the ravine with retrospective views of Grasmere and the lake.

Although the paths on either side of the huge mound of Great Tongue

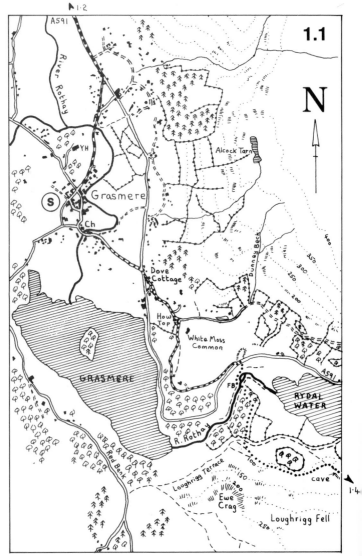

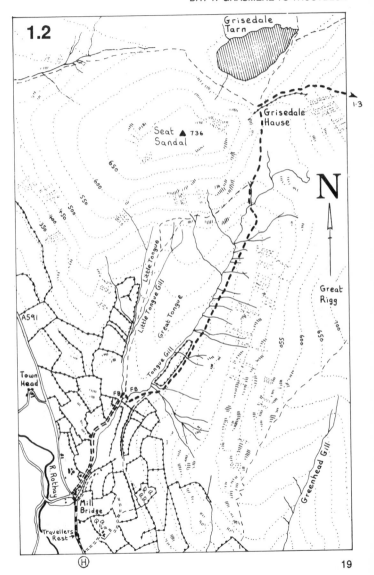

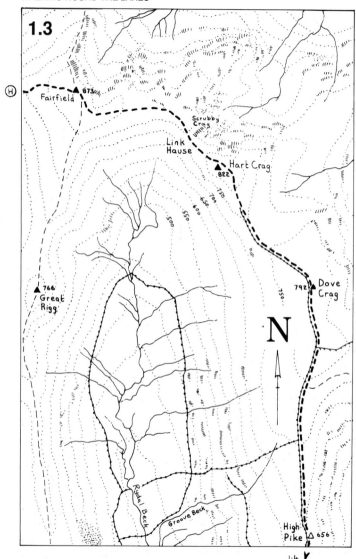

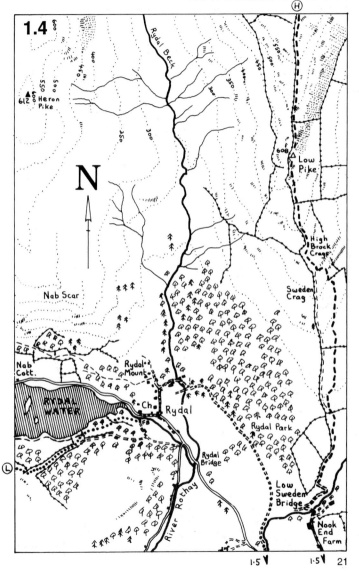

both lead to Grisedale Hause, the one to the right is the easier and has been restored by the National Trust. Crossing the two footbridges take the path climbing above Tongue Gill, where steep slopes on either hand rise to summits far above. To the right is Great Rigg while to the left Great Tongue buttresses the seldom visited Seat Sandal. Although little sign of them now remains, Great Tongue was the site of two iron ore mines, the Fairfield Mine and the Providence Mine. In the seventeenth century the ore was transported over Red Bank above Grasmere to Langdale for smelting and in the nineteenth century to Windermere station, but it was uneconomic and the mines closed in 1876.

After about a mile the route crosses the gill below a rocky cascade and then climbs to skirt Hause Moss before the final ascent to Grisedale Hause. Reaching the hause, **Grisedale Tarn** appears ahead, a tarn of many moods, but don't descend to it, instead turn right to follow the wall climbing towards Fairfield. Ahead in the Vee by Saint Sunday Crag is the first glimpse of Ullswater. Picking a route up the eroded scree slope, the cockscomb ridge of Striding Edge rising to Helvellyn forms the skyline across Grisedale, while on looking back the view expands to encompass the Coniston fells, the Langdale Pikes with Easedale Tarn in the foreground, Bow Fell and the Scafells, all to be visited in the course of the walk. As the angle eases, a good path materialises to the broad, flat and stony summit. The windshelter on the north-eastern edge high above Deepdale is the highest point of **Fairfield**. The fells on the eastern fringe of the Lake District are now in view and you can survey tomorrow's walk with the switchback of Yoke, Ill Bell and Froswick rising to Thornthwaite Beacon and High Street, then down past the glint of Angle Tarn into Patterdale.

The summit of Fairfield can be a confusing place in mist and care is needed to find the right way off. Follow the edge round to the south-east to pick up the good well-cairned path which ambles along dipping to Link Hause with Windermere ahead, before the short ascent to **Hart Crag**. The highest point is to the right of the path and is marked by a small cairn at the far end of the ridge. Below to the right, enclosed by the arms of the Fairfield Horseshoe, is the green empty valley of the Rydal Beck which in 1277 was surrounded by a stone wall with a ditch to form a natural hunting park.

The broad path joins a stone wall which is a close companion for the next few miles as it follows the ridge. **Dove Crag** is the next top, the summit is marked by a large cairn on a rock outcrop just to the left of the path. Although Helvellyn is hidden you can spot the point of Catstye Cam to the right of Striding Edge while north-eastwards Brothers Water and the foot of Ullswater are also to be seen.

Following the wall, the stone men at Bakestones away to the left look down on the Scandale valley and in the distance are High Raise and the scarp shape of Kidsty Pike. The ridge gradually descends towards the grassy prow of **High Pike** with Windermere beyond. Although prominent from the valley High Pike is only a momentary check in the smooth downward flow and no effort is needed for the neglible ascent to the cairn on the rocky knoll which marks the summit.

The wall continues towards Ambleside and a ladder stile is crossed to the final upthrust of the ridge at **Low Pike** where Rydal Water comes into view. Carry on descending beside the wall, then below High Brock Crags it is at last deserted to wander off downhill over bracken covered slopes and through fields. The path becomes a track crossing the Scandale Beck at Low Sweden Bridge to Nook End Farm. Nook Lane leads behind Charlotte Mason College into **Ambleside** where you turn right down Smithy Brow to join the main road then left onto the Low Level Route.

LOW LEVEL ROUTE

From the centre of **Grasmere** the road to the right of Sam Read's bookshop leads down to the church and the Gingerbread Shop. The shop was a tiny school built by public subscription in 1687 and William and Dorothy Wordsworth both gave lessons here. Entering the churchyard, a path beside the River Rothay leads to the eight yew trees which Wordsworth himself planted and the simple graves of the Wordsworth family. Rejoining the road, continue out to the A591 which neatly by-passes Grasmere and cross to the minor road passing **Dove Cottage**, the home of William and Dorothy for thirteen years.

Behind the cottage is the Grasmere and Wordsworth Museum. Opened in October 1981, it contains the original manuscripts of Dorothy's journals, some of Samuel Taylor Coleridge's work and also that of de Quincy, Scott and Sir Humphrey Davy, the inventor of the miners' safety lamp who was a friend of Wordsworth. Coleridge and the Wordsworths often used to meet at Thirlmere, the half-way point between their homes, and here they carved their initials on a rock. The rock, alas, was broken when it was moved during the construction of the reservoir, but Canon Rawnsley, the founder of the National Trust, gathered the pieces into a pyramid and in 1984 this 'Rock of Names' with its inscription 'WW MH TW STC JW SH' was moved to the quarry at the rear of the museum.

Looking back, the cottages on either hand form a frame for Helm Crag and the old turnpike road leads gently uphill away from the traffic to How Top with its tiny tarn. Turning right, signposted 'Rydal', the quiet little lane high above Grasmere rounds the hill. A path through a small iron gate into the wood joins the road further on which then descends past the rocky outcrops of **White Moss Common**. When the main road is joined at the car park in the quarry, which was worked until the new road was built in 1823, cross the A591 and walk upstream for a few yards to the footbridge. Crossing the River Rothay, the main path climbs straight on through the wood to a kissing gate and onto the open fellside. The track to Rydal Water turns left beside the wall,

Rydal Cave

but this misses **Rydal Quarry** with its huge cave, the largest in the Lake District. Instead go straight ahead climbing slightly and past a small wood to the cave, which produced an attractive decorative slate with ripple and raindrop patterns. On the spoil heap are the starry pink and white flowers of the English stonecrop and in the pool at the entrance minnows dart to and fro.

The quarry track descends past a second cave into the open above the lake where the lower path is joined. On the far shore of **Rydal Water** is Nab Cottage which was built in 1702 and this too has a connection with the Lake Poets for in 1816 de Quincy married the farmer's daughter, much to the disapproval of the Wordsworths. Later Hartley, the eldest son of Samuel Taylor Coleridge, lodged here for twelve years until his death in 1849.

The path beside the lake enters Rydal Woods through a kissing gate, then a little further on crosses the River Rothay at a footbridge where pink purslane and yellow irises flower in early summer. Again the road is reached, but after walking right for only a few yards turn left up the lane past Rydal Church, which was built by Lady le Fleming of Rydal Hall at a cost of £1,500 and opened on Christmas Day 1824. Behind the church is Dora's Field. Given by Wordsworth to his daughter, it now belongs to the National Trust and is a mass of daffodils in the spring. The steep lane leads to the sixteenth century farmhouse of **Rydal Mount** to which Wordsworth moved in 1813 with his family. The garden is unchanged and some of the original furniture

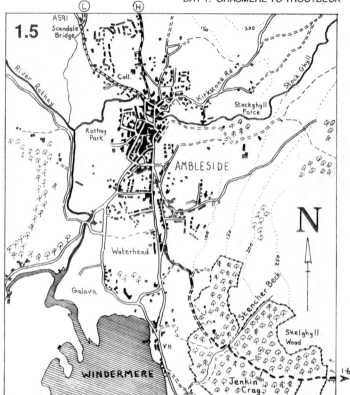

remains. Here he lived with his wife Mary and his sister Dorothy until his death in 1850. Although made Poet Laureate in 1843 by Queen Victoria, Wordsworth wrote nothing in his official capacity.

The second entrance on the right passes the private campsite and Youth Centre at the seventeenth century Rydal Hall whose garden is open to the public. The hall belongs to the Carlisle diocese of the Church of England and is a conference and study centre. The public footpath passes a tea shop, which appears never to open, and crosses Rydal Beck where the high stone wall on the right screens the gardens of the hall. The path forks right between the buildings then turns left along the track through the rhododendrons into **Rydal Park**, where the Fairfield Horseshoe Fell Race starts and finishes one Sunday in May.

After a mile you leave the park through a pair of magnificent wrought iron lodge gates and turn left along the busy main road past Charlotte Mason College into **Ambleside**.

AMBLESIDE

Thronging with people spilling off the pavements into the road and cars gyrating in the gigantic traffic roundabout, Ambleside is a hive of activity. With cafes and bookshops, outdoor pursuit shops and numerous giftshops, there is hardly any room for walkers.

Ambleside was originally a small mill village whose becks and rivers provided the power for the water-wheels. Stockghyll Force, a popular beauty spot from Victorian times, still has the remains of the railed viewpoints where Victorian ladies stood to admire the scene. Beside the stream, one of the old mills has been converted into holiday flats. In the centre of Ambleside the quaint little Bridge House, built over the River Rothay like something out of a fairy tale, dates from the seventeenth century and was painted by J.M.W.Turner. It was probably a summerhouse for Ambleside Hall and later in 1843 Chairy Rigg lived here with his wife and six children, though how they all fitted in is a mystery. In 1926 it was bought by the National Trust and in 1956 was its very first information and recruiting centre in the country.

JOINT ROUTE

The main A591 bends right by the Salutation Hotel where up to the left is Stockghyll Force, which is well worth the detour after heavy rain. Leaving Ambleside's fiendish one-way traffic system by Lake Road and just before the vast emporium of Hayes Garden Centre, turn up the narrow lane that runs behind the headquarters of the Langdale and Ambleside Mountain Rescue Team, one of the busiest mountain rescue teams in Britain. Climbing steadily away from the traffic again, the road becomes a track and contours along the slope high above Windermere with a bird's-eye view of the busy jetties at Waterhead. After passing Broad Ings, **Skelghyll Wood** is entered. The wood covers a narrow band of limestone which, interspersed with sand and mud, separates the Borrowdale Volcanics from the Skiddaw Slates. Shortly after entering the wood and forking left towards Jenkin (or Jenkyns) Crag and Troutbeck, the path first climbs beside and then crosses Stencher Beck. Briefly dividing into two, the paths rejoin before Kelsick Scar, which was presented to the National Trust by Alfred Holden Illingworth in memory of his wife in 1925. A few steps to the right is a grandstand view of busy Windermere from Jenkin Crag, a platform of andesite which is a rock of the Borrowdale Volcanics. In June you may find your clothes covered with looper caterpillars which hang down from the oak trees on threads.

Returning to the track continue through the wood towards Troutbeck. To the right is Dovenest Wood and the home of Felicia Hemans which is now a management centre. Not one of the Lake Poets and little-known, she lived from 1793 to 1835, and is now only remembered as the author of those famous lines: *The boy stood on the burning deck.* Below and hidden by the trees is Stagshaw Garden, a beautiful eight acres of exotic trees and shrubs with many rhododendrons and azaleas, and a lovely sight in the spring.

Leaving the trees the track continues to **High Skelghyll**. Below is Low Wood Hotel where speedboats and waterskiers from the water ski centre buzz around the lake. After the farm the lane becomes tarmac, passing through meadows which, with their many flowers, are more characteristic of the Dales than the Lake District. Forking left over Hol Beck to Troutbeck the bridleway climbs through the fields and past a ruin, fording a gill before turning right to Troutbeck at the Hundreds Road, an unsurfaced track.

There is no centre to Troutbeck, the youth hostel is at the southern end while the Mortal Man and some of the B & Bs are over two miles away at the northern end, so the last bit of the day depends on where you are staying.

For **Windermere Youth Hostel** take the second lane to the right which drops steeply down. Turn left and then fork right on the bridleway to descend again to join Bridge Lane, the road through the village. The youth hostel, a large house with extensive grounds, is half a mile to the right.

For the northern part of the village carry straight on along Robin Lane and past the cottages to enter **Troutbeck** by the post office and the Christadelphian Meeting Place. To the right 500 yards along the road is the National Trust property of Town End which is open to the public.

TROUTBECK

Over a mile from Town Head at its northern end to Town End in the south, with the youth hostel beyond even that, Troutbeck is the longest village in the Lakes. There is, however, no focus, no centre; even the church stands apart down on the main road and it is little more than a row of hamlets strung out along the hillside above the main road. Each is grouped round a series of wells which were built by the Dawson family and many of them are dedicated to saints. There is a post office in the village institute, which was built in 1869, the church and two pubs.

There are many 'statesman-plan farms' in Troutbeck which date from the seventeenth century and are made of local slate. A statesman, or estatesman, was originally a tenant farmer who had the right to pass on the tenancy to his children, but by the seventeenth century the statesmen had become freeholders. One of these farms is Town End which was built around 1626 and belonged to the Browne family until 1942. Because it was owned by the same family all the time, it has remained virtually unchanged. The house is divided into the 'down house' which is the farm and the 'fire house', the living quarters. It has mullioned windows and the tall cylindrical chimneys so characteristic of Westmorland. The house, which still contains the original

27

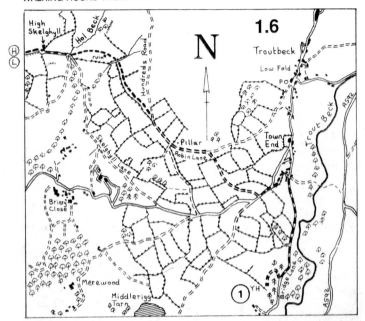

hand-made furniture, was given to the National Trust in 1944 and is open to the public.

There are also many bank-barns and the fine example opposite Town End is dated 1666. This was the Brownes' wool barn where fleeces were stacked before being sold and it has an unusual two-winged gallery. Bank-barns are two-storeyed buildings that are built on a slope. The hay was loaded into the upper part and it was then dropped down to the animals, sometimes the upper floor was used as a grain store or a threshing barn.

At the northern end of the village is the celebrated inn, The Mortal Man. Built in 1689 it was originally called the White Horse Inn, but was renamed at the beginning of the eighteenth century. It has an unusual signboard in verse:

> *O mortal man that lives by bread.*
> *What is it makes thy nose so red?*
> *Thou silly fool that looks so pale.*
> *Tis drinking Sally Birkett's ale.*

High Street

DAY 2 TROUTBECK TO PATTERDALE

HIGH LEVEL ROUTE	Distance 13 miles	Ascent 3,550ft
LOW LEVEL ROUTE	Distance 11 miles	Ascent 1,750ft

ROUTE SUMMARY

High Level Route After a steady plod up the ancient track of the Garburn Road the ridge is reached. The route is now indeed high-level, remaining above 1,500 feet for a delightful eight miles over the fells. The switchback ridge of Yoke, Ill Bell and Froswick leads to Thornthwaite Crag, then on, over High Street to descend gradually by Martindale Deer Forest, past Angle Tarn, and so down to Patterdale. It seems a long way and it is, but with good paths underfoot the ground is covered quickly to the head of Ullswater over much of the best of these Eastern Fells.

Low Level Route The quiet valley of Trout Beck climbs gradually to the high pass of Threshthwaite Mouth at almost 2,000ft where Pasture Beck leads down to the picturesque village of Hartsop with its spinning galleries and a final easy stroll to Patterdale.

NOTE: Whichever route is chosen, the other may be joined at Threshthwaite Mouth.

The Kentmere fells mark the boundary of the Lake District in character if not the one fixed by administrative man. Farther east the fells, although enclosed within the National Park, have the moorland feel of the Pennines rather than the dramatic rock scenery of the true Lake District, while the boundary of Cumbria stretches even farther east appropriating parts of the old counties of Yorkshire and Durham; but these Kentmere fells are still Lake District in form.

More often approached from the isolated village of Kentmere, the mountains which ring the head of the valley of the River Kent form an attractive horseshoe walk and the best bit is the traverse of the ridge from Yoke to Froswick over Ill Bell, the highest of this trio with the sentinel figure of Thornthwaite Beacon ahead on the skyline.

This magnificent fourteen-foot stone column means there can be no mistaking where you are, or so we thought until we met a puzzled group who had identified it as Mardale Ill Bell - which is a good mile away to the east!

Beyond Thornthwaite Crag is High Street where once the Romans trod when the valleys were still thick forest and safety from ambush lay in keeping to the high ground from which they could look down on their enemies. Built on the route of a prehistoric trackway this Roman road ran from Brocavum near Penrith to Galava at Ambleside high above the boggy wooded valleys, but long after High Street lost its importance as a highway with the opening up of the valley routes, the fell acquired a new and unusual function. An annual shepherds' fair was held on July 12 to reclaim stray sheep and there was horse racing, wrestling and games. High Street was known as Racecourse Hill and is still so named on the OS map, although the last meeting was held here in 1835.

The featureless High Street plateau can be confusing in mist, though having gained the summit the concrete OS trig point leaves your position in no doubt. Walking along the broad green ridge, its flat grassy top gives no hint of the rock scenery close at hand, but the eastern edge drops via the rocky ridge of Rough Crag to Haweswater. This quiet valley is remembered with affection by all those who knew it before Manchester Corporation got its hands on it and built a 120-foot high dam to form a reservoir. Work started in 1929 and the reservoir was opened in 1940. The little village of Mardale was drowned and in times of drought, when the water level is low, the outline of its walls can be seen again. The seventeenth-century Dun Bull Inn has been replaced by the Haweswater Hotel which has been built half-way down the lake in the middle of nowhere. Haweswater is fed by underground pipes from Ullswater which, after a long fight in Parliament, has remained unspoiled.

Beneath Rough Crag, Blea Water and the lovely Small Water are set high in the fells in rocky hollows, formed at the head of the glacier which once filled the main valley. The crags above Blea Water are one of the few favoured places where the generally acid rock gives way to rocks with a slightly higher lime content and here some of the rarer mountain plants can be found clinging to ledges out of reach of even the agile sheep.

Angle Tarn, more open in aspect than its namesake in the Central Fells, and more often reflecting the sun, is a good place for a rest before leaving the mountains behind to descend to Boredale Hause and Patterdale.

At Boredale Hause are the remains of a medieval chapel which was built to serve the people of both Martindale and Patterdale. Before we knew of its origins, we once irreverently sat upon the stones to eat our lunch. Wordsworth mentions it in his *Guide to the Lakes* which was published in its final version in 1835:

A small ruin, called at this day the chapel, where it is said the inhabitants of Martindale and Patterdale were accustomed to assemble for worship. There are now no traces from which you could infer for what use the building had been erected; the loose stones and the few which yet continue piled up resemble those which lie elsewhere on the mountain; but the shape of the building having been oblong, its remains differ from those of a common sheep-fold; and it has stood east and west.

His description of the descent from the hause remains unchanged:
As we descend, Patterdale opens upon the eye in grand simplicity,

31

screened by mountains, and proceeding from two heads, Deepdale and Hartshope, where lies the little lake of Brotherswater, named in old maps Broaderwater,....but the change in the appelation of this small lake or pool (if it be a corruption) may have been assisted by some melancholy accident similar to what happened about twenty years ago, when two brothers were drowned there, having gone out to take their holiday pleasure upon the ice on a new-year's day.

The little freqented Trout Beck valley makes an easy pathway through the fells. An isolated lump of hillside, the Tongue, almost blocks the end, but Trout Beck, a river in size if not in name, squeezes past in a series of falls, spectacular after heavy rain. Hunched below the Tongue is Troutbeck Park, a remote sheep farm dating from medieval days when this whole area was a deer park enclosed by a high wall. The farm and land were bought by Beatrix Potter in 1924 when it was in a very neglected state. Here she farmed her favourite Herdwicks. These are small sturdy animals with a very coarse wool, agile and hardy and well suited to the Lake District terrain. Hornless with white or grey faces they have pleasant expressions and can be easily identified in the spring as their lambs are born black. Herdwicks were probably originally brought to England from Norway by the conquering Norsemen. With nearly 2,000 acres Troutbeck Park is one of the most famous sheep farms in the Lake District and now belongs to the National Trust.

Much of Beatrix Potter's little known book *The Fairy Caravan* is set around Troutbeck Park. Less popular than her other books, this tells the story of a travelling circus troupe of animals and is a collection of short tales. Billy the pony trots over Ings Bridge and another of the illustrations is of the farm and the sheepdogs among the hills that she loved so well.

ROUTE DESCRIPTION

HIGH LEVEL ROUTE

From Windermere Youth Hostel walk north up the road as far as **Troutbeck** Post Office then take the lane opposite which descends to the A592. Turn left past Jesus Church, which dates from the end of the fifteenth century and was enlarged in 1736, and then right into Limefitt Park, a large campsite and also a grass ski centre. The bridleway passes through the campsite and going between the buildings a track leads out to join another heading up the valley. Crossing straight over, a small path climbs steeply to join the old **Garburn Road** below Applethwaite Quarry. Across the valley and strung out in a long line on the hillside are the houses and farms of Troutbeck and towards the head of the valley is the low mound of The Tongue with the National Trust farm of Troutbeck Park at its foot . Beyond are the higher fells. The dip in the skyline is Threshthwaite Mouth with Thornthwaite Beacon and the ridge of

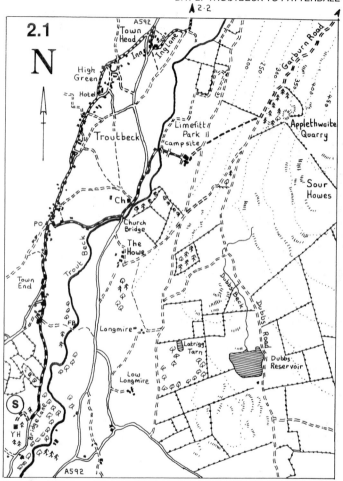

Froswick, Ill Bell and Yoke to the right .

The old packhorse route climbs steadily between walls composed of a mixture of hard rocks and softer shales which have crumbled away to nothing in places causing the wall to collapse. This is a geological junction of two rock types with the Borrowdale volcanics to the north and the Silurian shales to the south. At the summit of **Garburn Pass** in a little over a mile, geological

33

Trout Beck

maps show the narrow band of Coniston Limestone outcropping again as it does at Skelghyll Wood.

Turn left to follow the wall up grassy slopes towards Yoke, the first mountain of the day. The path, which can be boggy at first, stays beside the wall for about a mile until a ladder stile is reached at the wall corner. Continue steeply up to the ridge where a final plod leads to the top of **Yoke** which has a small cairn on a rocky rib in the middle of a grassy expanse.

Walking along the grassy ridge an occasional distant boom may be heard from Pets Quarry, the huge gash on the side of Red Screes away to the left where stone is still being quarried. Ahead is Ill Bell and High Street and to the right is Nan Bield Pass which separates the western hills of the Kentmere Horseshoe from Harter Fell.

Ill Bell looks a lot higher but is soon reached. This attractive summit with its outcropping rock has two large cairns laying claim to be the top, but both are in fact of equal height. To the west is the quiet valley of Trout Beck, the line taken by the Low Route, and ahead on the skyline to the left of Froswick is the tall cairn of Thornthwaite Beacon. Beyond is High Street, while a stroll to the eastern edge reveals Kentmere Reservoir and the Kentmere valley looking a long way below. The reservoir was constructed at the end of the last century to provide a constant head of water for the ninety mills powered by the River Kent which rises in Hall Cove just above. In 25 miles the river drops 1,000 feet and is reputed to be the swiftest in the country.

Directly ahead is a steep drop to Over Cove and the path swings away left, but after an initially stony descent over flat slabs, easy grass slopes are followed by a straightforward climb to **Froswick** which has a cairn on the small top. Again there is a bird's-eye view of Kentmere Reservoir with Harter Fell and Kentmere Pike across the valley.

There is not too much loss of height on the next section as the path dips to the col above pink screes which fall towards the River Kent. A steady grassy climb follows and at an old iron fence straining post, fork left to the beacon which vanishes from sight as you approach. **Thornthwaite Crag** has a fine stone column set upon the wall corner. To the west lies Stony Cove Pike on the other side of Threshthwaite Mouth.

A short cut can be taken here to avoid High Street by following the wall down to Threshthwaite Mouth to join the Low Level Route.

A broad path, with views down to Hayes Water, sweeps round the head of the valley to the corner of a ruined stone wall. The path which continues to the left of the wall is the line of the old Roman road, but the Romans, who obviously weren't into peak bagging, built their road by-passing the summit. However, the wall heads north over High Street leading directly to the top and by following it the concrete OS trig point, which stands on the summit of **High Street**, is soon reached. The ground is too flat for this to be a good viewpoint, though to the west the full extent of the Helvellyn range can be admired with the Scafells and the Coniston fells further away. Although it is so flat, the eastern slopes of High Street fall steeply and roughly to Haweswater, the white shoreline giving it an artificial appearance and you should not miss the short stroll to the eastern edge which brings Blea Water, the deepest tarn in the Lake District, into view hidden in its little combe. The long, high ridge away to the east is the Pennines and in clear conditions you can identify Cross Fell, the Howgills and the Yorkshire hills.

Follow the wall down from the summit with the line of the old Roman road to the left and on reaching the col, the Straits of Riggindale, you look down the long deserted valley of Riggindale. In recent years Golden Eagles have been reintroduced and are again breeding in this valley, watched over day and night by protective wardens. Forking left at the col continue on the main path climbing beside the wall which turns left for a few final feet of ascent to **The Knott** with its cairn constructed of stones from the ruined wall. Just

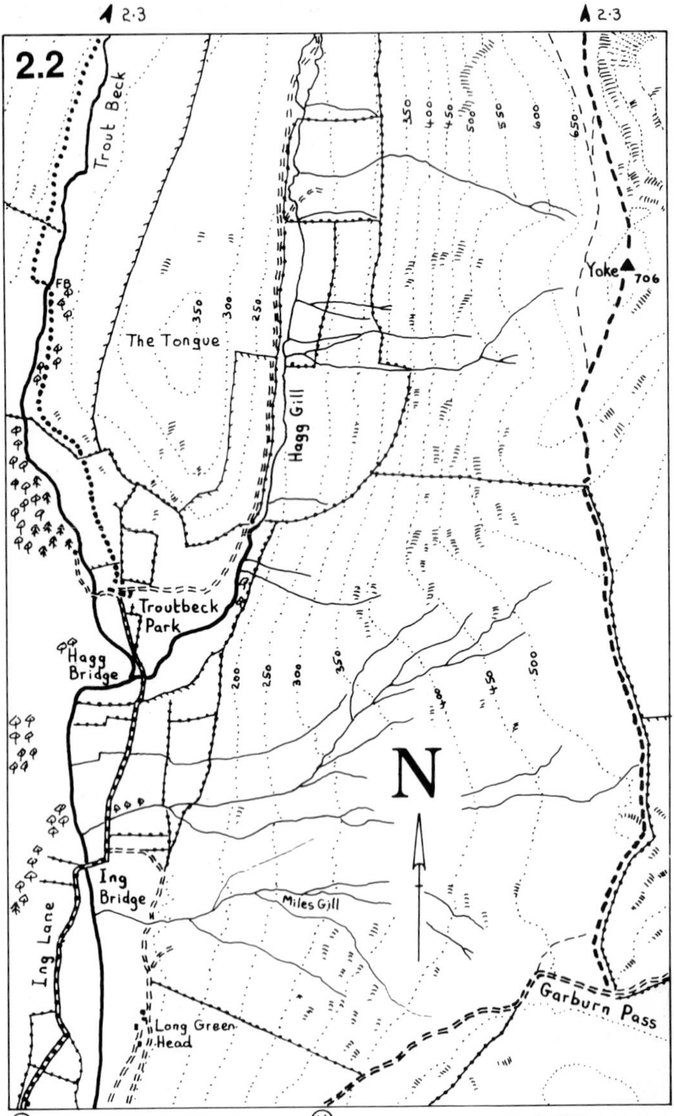
2·3
2·3
2.2
Trout Beck
FB
The Tongue
Hagg Gill
350
300
250
350
400
450
500
550
600
650
Yoke
706
Troutbeck
Park
Hagg
Bridge
200
250
300
350
400
450
500
N
Ing
Bridge
Miles Gill
Ing Lane
Long Green
Head
Garburn Pass
L
H

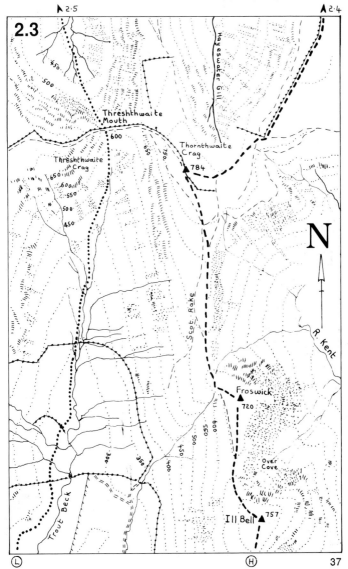

Froswick and Ill Bell

beyond the cairn Hayes Water comes into view and on the far side of the empty valley is the Gray Crag ridge. To the north the long High Street ridge stretches for another 4 miles to the final outpost of Loadpot Hill.

Follow the wall down over grass to rejoin the main path. The wall continues almost to the top of Rest Dodd and beyond is The Nab where 300 red deer are preserved and protected. There have been deer on the Nab continuously since medieval times when they were to be found on all the fells. Down in Martindale you briefly glimpse the red roof of The Bungalow which was originally a Victorian hunting lodge. It was used to house officers during the war and more recently was let as furnished holiday accommodation. Ahead, beyond Hartsop village, lies Brothers Water. The path crosses a boggy area below the grassy cone of Rest Dodd and then follows a fence round and after sweeping views northwards down the length of Bannerdale, a small gate is reached.

Cresting the rise, below is **Angle Tarn**. The path descends to the tarn and rounds it on the far side. The path divides, only to rejoin further on, but the left fork follows the more attractive route which becomes a little alpine trod curving round the edge of the hillside. The clear path continues down to **Boredale Hause** where the remains of the medieval Chapel in the Hause a little further over may be easily mistaken for a sheep fold. Cross Stonebarrow Gill and take the main path north-west which slants down across the hillside towards the head of Ullswater. Turn left onto the tarmac road, then join the Low Level Route at the junction for the last few yards into **Patterdale**.

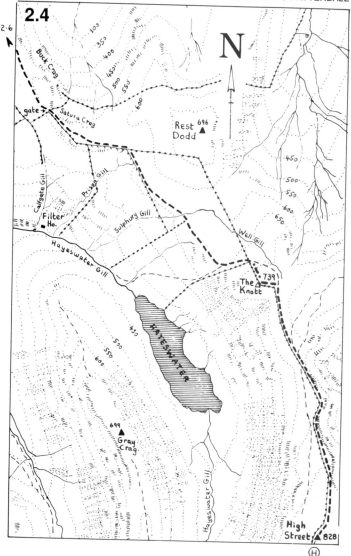

2.4

2·6

Buck Crag

gate

Satura Crag

N

Rest Dodd 696 ▲

300
350
400
450
500
550
600

450
500
550
600
650

Cauldgate Gill

Prison Gill

Filter Ho.

Sulphury Gill

Hayeswater Gill

Well Gill

The Knott ▲ 739

HAYESWATER

450
550
600

Gray Crag 699 ▲

Hayeswater Gill

High Street ▲ 828

Ⓗ

39

Angle Tarn

LOW LEVEL ROUTE

From Windermere Youth Hostel take the road north through the scattered hamlets of **Troutbeck** village, past the seventeenth-century statesman-house of Town End and the post office, for a couple of miles to Town Head. The wells by the roadside are dedicated to various saints, with 'Saint John's Well' and 'Saint James's Well' followed by 'Margaret's Well'. From the elevated road there are wide views over the Trout Beck valley. The lane by-passes the Mortal Man at High Green before descending to the A592. Cross the main road and go down the lane to the farms and cottages of **Town Head** and after 100 yards turn left along Ing Lane which is a private road.

This traffic-free tarmac lane makes easy work of the mile-and-a-half to **Troutbeck Park**, which was one of the fourteen Lakeland Herdwick sheep farms bequeathed to the National Trust by Beatrix Potter on her death in 1943. As we walked up the road with its flower-strewn verge we came suddenly on a ghostly spectre, a tree shrouded with a grey web, every inch covered with heaving clingfilm. They were Lesser Ermine Moth caterpillars which live communally in 'tents' often killing the hawthorn or sloe bush on which they are feeding.

Continuing up the road, foxgloves, cranesbill and dog roses brighten the flat valley floor and beyond the farm The Tongue, an isolated lump of fellside, rises strangely in the middle of the valley. Passing to the left of the farm buildings the waymarked path follows a rough track to the right of the beck, but turns into a rather boggy footpath through the trees. Keeping uphill to avoid the juiciest bits, the path crosses the Trout Beck above a series of falls

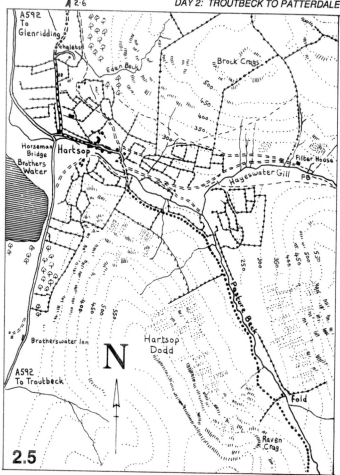

by an immensely broad clapper bridge built around 1650. The path now continues for a good 2 miles, climbing almost imperceptably up the wide empty valley. Gradually the valley closes in and the path steepens, with Froswick and Ill Bell on the skyline high above to the right. On the flanks of Froswick the slanting path of the old Roman road can clearly be seen climbing up the fell. Known locally as Scot Rake it is reputed to be the route

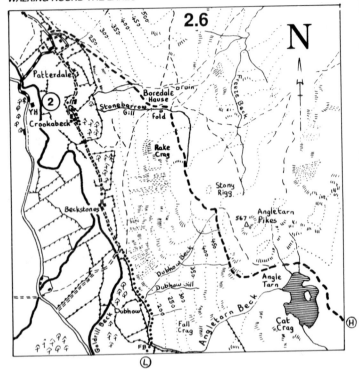

taken by marauding Scottish raiders.

As the ground steepens the beck disappears into a narrow little gorge. Crossing above a water spout beyond the gorge, a path climbs the grassy tongue between the two streams, then picks its way through the boulders on the left of the valley to another grassy strip and the col at **Threshthwaite Mouth**. The gentle slopes of the Troutbeck valley are now replaced by the rugged contours of the fells ahead and beyond is Ullswater gleaming in the distance with Place Fell standing proudly to its right.

The High Level Route may be joined at this point by following the wall from the col to the summit of Thornthwaite Crag.

Continuing straight over the col and now much more obvious, the path descends into Threshthwaite Cove, to the left of the meandering Pasture Beck, before dropping again to the left of the ravine which the stream has carved out for itself. The path continues past giant boulders to Pasture

Bottom. This typically U-shaped stepped glacial valley has mounds of debris left by the retreating ice and the beck deepens to pebble-bottomed pools before joining Hayes Water Gill by old lead mine workings. Worked from 1867 to around 1878 the mine was troubled by flooding and remains of the water course supports and the pit, which housed a 30-foot water wheel, can still be seen.

A good broad track leads down to the village of **Hartsop**, where Pasture Beck is crossed at Walker Bridge. The land around here was once a hunting forest. Many of the buildings date from the seventeenth century and there are two spinning galleries. These are covered balconies where the wool from the local Herdwick sheep was spun in the open air to make the maximum use of the daylight when the cottage industry was at its peak. Walk through the village nearly to the main road (where there is a telephone box) and turn right on the tarmac lane. The tarmac is for the benefit of the occupants of the holiday chalets at Hartsop Fold, but continue beyond the chalets on the rough track to the footbridge over Angletarn Beck. There are attractive falls just above. The good path climbs a little and an extra spurt of energy is needed to make the metal seat above the track for a fine prospect of Brothers Water. It is not far now, just follow the main track to the right of Goldrill Beck past Beckstones farm and gently downhill for the final mile to Patterdale. A permissive footpath avoids Crookabeck, rejoining the track further on. Finally turn left at the T-junction to join the High Level Route for the last few yards into **Patterdale** village.

PATTERDALE

The loveliest aspect of Patterdale is its position at the head of Ullswater. Standing away from the lake and surrounded by mountains there cannot be many more attractive spots in the whole of Lakeland. On the far side of Goldrill Beck a cluster of houses and farms has crept away from the main road and shelter under Place Fell, but there isn't much to the village save the youth hostel, the White Lion, the post office and the snack bar. Happily the school, which was built in 1873, is still thriving.

The dale is supposedly named after Saint Patrick who came to England from Ireland at the beginning of the fifth century to spread the Christian faith in mountainous areas. After being shipwrecked he passed through this valley on his travels through Celtic Britain and on the main road towards Glenridding is Saint Patrick's Well, a holy well reputed to have healing properties where Saint Patrick baptised the local people. However, a much more likely explanation is that the name comes from a Norseman named Patriac who came over from Ireland in the tenth century and settled here.

During the first half of the nineteenth century the population of Patterdale trebled because of the mining boom. A new church was built in 1853 to replace an earlier medieval chapel and now in the spring the daffodils in the churchyard rival the more famous ones at Grasmere. Inside the church there is a communion plate and a chalice made of silver mined below Helvellyn, which were presented to the church in 1850 by the Greenside Mining Company. In 1890 this was the first church in the country to be lit with electric light, also provided by the mining company. The church warden's staves are the work of Robert Thompson of Kilburn, Yorkshire, and are easily identified by his trademark, a carved wooden mouse. Nearly opposite Saint Patrick's church stands the fire station with its shiny red fire engine.

Every winter some of the Martindale red deer migrate to Patterdale to find new pastures, straying onto the slopes of Place Fell. This is one of the two major deer herds in the Lakes, the other being in Grizedale to the south. There have been deer here since the Middle Ages and walkers are discouraged from venturing onto their preserve in Martindale and Bannerdale. Although they have been managed, they are not fed and in very bad weather they come down to the village when you may see them on the slopes below Boredale Hause.

John - winter backpacking on High Street

Striding Edge

DAY 3 PATTERDALE TO GLENRIDDING

HIGH LEVEL ROUTE	Distance 6½ miles	Ascent 3,050ft
LOW LEVEL ROUTE		
Lanty's Tarn	Distance 4 miles	Ascent 1,000ft
Red Tarn	Distance 5 miles	Ascent 2,000ft

ROUTE SUMMARY

High Level Route One of the finest ways to a mountain top in the country, the narrow rocky ridge of Striding Edge leads to Helvellyn and the return down Swirral Edge completes a classic Lake District round. Though not strenuous or difficult for the average walker, the rate of progress along both edges is slow.

Low Level Route The easiest day of the whole tour. A gentle stroll to Lanty's Tarn is followed by an afternoon relaxing at Glenridding with perhaps a steamer trip on Ullswater.

NOTE: A more energetic alternative is to follow the High Level Route to Hole-in-the-Wall and then descend by way of Red Tarn.

Although of all the Lake District's 3,000ft mountains Helvellyn is not the highest, it is nevertheless the one for which most people hold the greatest affection. The lure of Striding Edge is certainly part of the explanation for if all the approaches to the top were by way of the mountain's rounded grassy western slopes, then there would be little save height to distinguish Helvellyn from many another Lakeland objective. Yet it cannot just be the thrill of scrambling along the narrow eastern edges that attracts the crowds, for the western slopes are crossed by broad highways up which the pilgrims plod. For many people this must be their first approach as it was ours, and it was also up these slopes that we carried one of the children to his first 3,000-foot summit. But having reached the broad flat top of loose stones and patchy grass, you walk across to the trig point and look down into the eastern combe. The eastern side is a shock. There are no grassy slopes here, but the mountain falls away uncompromisingly and precipitously to Red Tarn over 800 feet below. On either hand, enfolding the tarn and stretching out towards Ullswater, are two narrow arêtes, Swirral Edge and Striding Edge, sharpened to a fine crest by the opposing forces of the glaciers that carved these eastern combes. This is the wild side of the mountain and having seen this view who does not instantly fall in love with Helvellyn and who will not return again and again?

While westward the panorama is all of mountains, Bow Fell, Pillar, Gable and the Scafells, eastwards the scene stretches uninterrupted across the

46

much lower fells of Martindale and Shap to the distant Pennines and it is this unobstructed view that makes Helvellyn a favourite spot from which to watch the sunrise. In midsummer this is at an early hour indeed and most people spend the short hours of darkness bivouacking uncomfortably in the wall shelter watching the gradually lightening eastern sky.

There are better ways of doing it. We arrived on the summit late one June afternoon and pitched our tent beside the trig point on the very top. Setting the alarm for what we hoped was a suitably early hour, we rose rather too early, and then watched entranced as the first flicker of dawn grew to the orange disc of the sun whose rays touched in turn each of the blue-grey silhouettes of the mountains setting them aflame with light.

Winter too brings a special magic to the sunrise. The early start is out as the sun rises at a very civilised hour and while camping on the tops in midwinter is a very much more serious adventure, the crystal clear views are unmatched. If the ground is so hard that pegs buckle as they are hammered in, and if the water bottle freezes solid, it's worth it for the mystical experience of seeing the creation of the world from black night into brilliant day.

On a summer weekend the summit plateau can seem almost as busy as the towns and villages. From every direction they come. Some, even in a heatwave, in anoraks, boots and gaiters, some in shorts and trainers and some in beachwear carrying shopping bags as if by a miracle they had been whisked from the centre of Ambleside to this Lakeland summit. One enthusiast we met had erected a tall radio mast on the summit and told us he had talked for twenty minutes on some impossibly high radio frequency with another radio ham in Spain. A few are less enthusiastic, like the party of teenagers trudging silently uphill in low cloud and drizzle. "Keep it goin' Julie, one step at a time," called their instructor, informing us they were being taken "for a little navigation". Heads down, they plodded miserably on into the wet seeing nothing but the vanishing heels of the one in front while we went to look at the memorials.

There are two memorials on the summit of Helvellyn, one to an aeroplane and one to a dog. On the broad path to Nethermost Pike is a plaque commemorating the fact that: *The first aeroplane to land on a mountain in Great Britain did so on this spot on December 22nd 1926*. The other memorial, erected by Canon Rawnsley, is sited where Striding Edge abuts Helvellyn and commemorates a dog who stayed by his master's body for three months after he fell to his death in a snowstorm. This story is recorded by Wordsworth in his *Guide to the Lakes* when he is describing Red Tarn.

A silent tarn in the recesses of Helvellyn. This desolate spot was formerly haunted by eagles that built in the precipice which forms its western barrier. It also derives a melancholy interest from the fate of a young man, a stranger, who perished some years ago, by falling down the rocks in his attempt to cross over to Grasmere. His remains

47

Winter on the summit of Helvellyn

were discovered by means of a faithful dog that had lingered here for the space of three months, self-supported, and probably retaining to the last an attachment to the skeleton of its master.

Wordsworth climbed Helvellyn later the same year with Walter Scott and the chemist Humphrey Davy. The two poets were much moved by the event and each wrote a poem not knowing that the other was doing the same thing. Wordsworth recorded it in his lines on *Fidelity* which are inscribed on the plaque while Walter Scott described it in *I climbed the dark brow of the mighty Helvellyn*:

How long didst thou think that his silence was slumber?
When the wind waved his garment how oft didst thou start?

Although mist is no deterrent to the traverse of Striding Edge, and it would be difficult indeed to get lost, high winds, torrential rain or ice and snow should all lead to a choice of the Low Route. Today is the least strenuous of all the days on this walk ,so make the most of it. Lie in, get up slowly, savour the pleasure that no matter how late you start there will be plenty of time. Morning coffee in Patterdale, lunch by Lanty's Tarn followed by a cream tea in Glenridding and a visit to the National Park information centre will nicely fill up the day.

Just above Lanty's Tarn is Keldas, a rocky pine-clad promontory which is a marvellous viewpoint for Ullswater, one of the Lake District's most

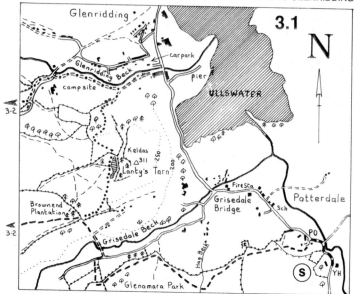

beautiful lakes. Unlike the rest of the major lakes which are essentially straight, Ullswater is almost serpentine in shape with three distinct sections. This is thought to be due to a sequence of glaciers each of which carved out a different channel. The head of the lake is the most dramatic, surrounded by mountains formed from the Borrowdale Volcanic rocks, the centre section is the Skiddaw Slates and these give way in turn to limestone and sandstone towards the foot of the lake at Pooley Bridge. Ullswater is a public highway with a speed limit of 10mph and a steamer service regularly circles the lake starting from the pier at Glenridding, a beautiful journey in delectable surroundings.

ROUTE DESCRIPTION

JOINT ROUTE

Opposite the White Lion in **Patterdale** a track leads round behind the buildings to a marshy tarn and the path to Grisedale. The path crosses the stream, goes through a kissing gate and then wanders along the bottom of the fell through Glenamara Park. Crossing Hag Beck it then rounds the foot of Birks, that outlier of Saint Sunday Crag which means Birch Tree Fell, and, keeping above the larch plantation, continues beside the wall. Reaching some

49

sheepfolds beyond a kissing gate, turn right to drop down through the fields to the left of a barn and out to the lane. Go right on the lane and then immediately left after the gate, signed 'Footpath to Helvellyn', to cross Grisedale Beck. The loud yelps, barks and howls come from the building to the right, the home of the Ullswater Foxhounds. At the bend, leave the track to climb straight up the field and through the gate below Brownend Plantation where the High and Low Routes divide.

HIGH LEVEL ROUTE

Turn left taking the higher path which climbs steadily for 1½ miles with a final steep section up to **Hole-in-the-Wall**. If on gaining the ridge the weather has worsened a short cut can be taken, leaving out Helvellyn and Catstye Cam, by descending gently to Red Tarn to join the return route.

The main path would be difficult to miss in anything like good weather with a steady procession of enthusiastic walkers bound for Striding Edge. Below is Red Tarn, the only tarn in the Lake District in which the schelly or freshwater herring is found, though it also lives in two of the lakes, Ullswater and Haweswater. The summit of **Striding Edge** is the rocky point known as High Spying How at the eastern end, but it is a few feet above the path and is frequently missed. Just after the highest point is a memorial, a metal plaque on a little platform. The faded inscription is now almost illegible:

> In memory of Robert Dixon, Rookings, Patterdale, who was killed on this place on the 27th day of November 1858 when following the Patterdale foxhounds.

The edge, which seems narrow enough, especially in less than perfect conditions, would be a far more daunting experience if the loose rock which covers its sides was stripped away, as under this mantle the glaciers have honed the ridge to a thin sliver of rock. Although for some it is a matter of pride to stick to the very crest, most people opt for the path which stays a little below it on the right. The end of the ridge presents the greatest difficulty, a short but steep scramble down the rocks, but this also can be avoided by a path below on the left of the ridge. A rough scramble follows, up scree and rock to emerge by the Gough Memorial, almost on the summit.

> Beneath this spot were found in 1805 the remains of Charles Gough, killed by a fall from the rocks. His dog was still guarding the skeleton. In memory of that love & strength of feeling this stone is erected 1890

Follow the edge round to the four-bay wind shelter which was rebuilt in 1968, and just beyond is a large untidy cairn which is, in fact, the highest point of **Helvellyn** and higher than the OS trig point a little beyond. The summit is an almost flat expanse of small stones with the trig point on the edge overlooking Red Tarn. In winter a cornice forms along the rim, a trap for incautious walkers who venture too close. The top is always busy with people

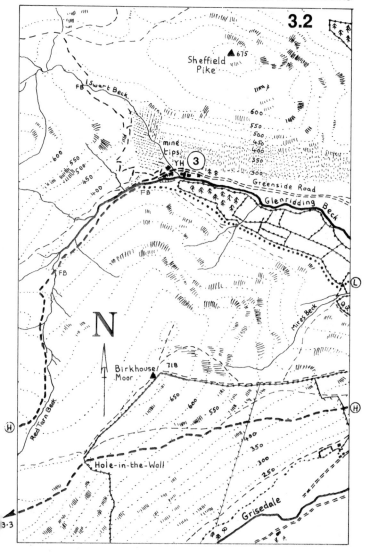

Anne and Joe climbing Catstye Cam

as Helvellyn is probably the most popular of all the Lake District mountains. It is the highest in England after the Scafells and if you are fortunate enough to have a good seeing day nearly every fell to be climbed on the tour is in view. Red Tarn in its glacial combe is encircled by the two arms of Swirral and Striding Edges, eastward the view extends over the lowland of the Shap fells to the Pennines some thirty miles away, and all around more than a hundred Lakeland fells are to be seen.

Continue along the edge to a small cemented cairn which marks the start of the steep but easy descent down the narrow crest of **Swirral Edge**. From the lowest point on the ridge a path slants right and down towards Red Tarn, which, though it was enlarged in 1860 to supply water to the Greenside Mine, is now back to its original level. Continue along the ridge climbing quite steeply up the cone of **Catstye Cam**, which means steep wild cat ridge path, to the small cairn marking the highest point. Across the valley to the left the Helvellyn ridge stretches northwards over the Dodds, tomorrow's expedition, and below is Keppel Cove where in the middle of a stormy night in October 1927 the reservoir earth dam burst, causing a flood of water to sweep down upon Glenridding. Miraculously no lives were lost, but a peninsula of debris was left jutting out into Ullswater and on this the steamer pier was built.

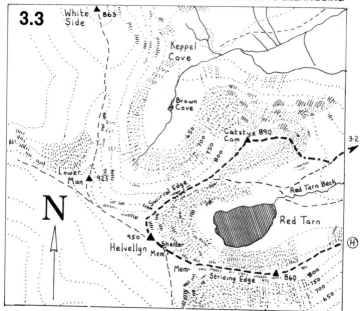

Descending at first gradually, the ridge heads east and then a cairned path zigzags down through a stony section, becoming indistinct on reaching the grass. Continue in the same direction to join the good path which descends beside Red Tarn Beck to a footbridge and then an iron bridge is reached at the site of the old Greenside Lead Mine where one of the mine buildings on the other side of the stream is now the **Helvellyn Youth Hostel**.

More luxurious accommodation is available in Glenridding itself 1¹/₂ miles down Greenside Road, but to avoid the road walking the Low Level Route can be followed down to the valley. Don't cross the iron bridge but, staying on the path on the right of Glenridding Beck, keep just above the wall, the path being less obvious than the higher one which follows an old leat which was the head race to the 1928 village power station at Rattlebeck. Across the river you can see the huge scar of the old workings above the mine buildings and in the hard-won fields of the valley floor are heaps of stones collected when the land was cleared. In a mile cross the ladder stile and then go down a rough track to turn right just before Rattlebeck Bridge. The path goes through the campsite and beside the river to **Glenridding** village.

Lanty's Tarn

LOW LEVEL ROUTE

Turn right through the kissing gate below Brownend Plantation and follow the higher track to Glenridding. The good path crosses the hillside to climb to **Lanty's Tarn** which is enclosed by woodland. This was named after Lancelot Dobson who lived in a large house in the valley below and owned most of Grisedale.

From the kissing gate at the northern end of the tarn the route descends into Glenridding. To the right is the little hill of **Keldas**, a magnificent viewpoint overlooking Ullswater. The main path zigzags down to a wood then past some cottages to a track. Turn right beside Glenridding Beck for **Glenridding** village and the shores of the lake or left to go directly to Helvellyn Youth Hostel.

For the youth hostel stay beside the beck signed 'Gillside Farm and Greenside' through the campsite, then turn left on the rough track beyond signed 'Greenside' and climb to a ladder stile onto the open fellside. A clear path to Greenside Mine follows the intake wall for a mile to a metal bridge above **Helvellyn Youth Hostel**.

If the afternoon has been spent in Glenridding, Helvellyn Youth Hostel may also be reached by following the road to the right of Glenridding Beck past the houses and the Traveller's Rest, then turning right along Greenside Road which leads up to the old mines and the hostel.

GLENRIDDING

Glenridding, like Patterdale, is a mining village, a rather unattractive collection of houses, but a beautiful setting. Pride of place is given to an enormous car park, a National Park information centre and a toilet block. There are a couple of food stores and an outdoor pursuit shop. It is a good idea to stock up with provisions here or check that tomorrow's shop, the post office at Threlkeld, will be open. The houses straggle up the hillside towards Greenside Mine where the former home of the mine manager is now Helvellyn Youth Hostel.

From the pier which juts into Ullswater two nineteenth century steamers, fitted with diesel engines in the 1930s, cruise the seven-mile lake to Pooley Bridge and Howtown. The *Lady of the Lake* was launched in 1877 and *The Raven* was completed in 1889.

Glenridding developed as a mining village in the middle of the nineteenth century when around 300 workers were employed at Greenside Mine, mostly as lead miners and smelters. Many of the workers came from Alston and Coniston and lodged for the week, going home at weekends. Some even made the journey from Alston on foot, a round trip of nearly 70 miles.

First discovered by the Romans, Greenside Mine has been worked for lead since the middle of the eighteenth century and in the nineteenth century it was one of the most important mines in the Lake District. The mine produced 2,500 tons of ore in a month yielding 150 tons of lead concentrates, the remainder was waste or tailings and this was dumped producing the unsightly spoil heaps we see today. Attempts have been made to grow vegetation on the waste and many of the huge scars are now greened over.

The earliest levels were those highest up the fell towards the Helvellyn ridge and the later levels were mined progressively lower down and deeper into the hillside. The main crushing and smelting mills were built towards the end of the 1850s in the valley near the site of the present Helvellyn Youth Hostel and the smelting mill had a $1\frac{1}{2}$-mile long flue which led to a chimney on the slopes of Raise. Around 1860 Red Tarn was enlarged along with other nearby tarns to provide water power for these mills, seven tons of water being needed for every ton of extracted ore. The water-wheels were soon replaced by turbines and in 1891 electrical haulage was introduced. Greenside was the first mine in Britain to have electrical winding gear at the top of the shaft and it was also, in 1893, the first to have an electrical locomotive in a mine, though ponies were also used until 1945.

During the Second World War Greenside Mine provided 80 per cent of all the lead mined in the country. It was worked by Italian prisoners of war from South Africa and the ore was taken to Newcastle by road for smelting. The mine which had operated for around 200 years, finally closed in 1962. After this the Atomic Energy Authority used it to make an underground explosion in order to test the instruments used to detect underground nuclear explosions, but all is now quiet again with nature healing the scars.

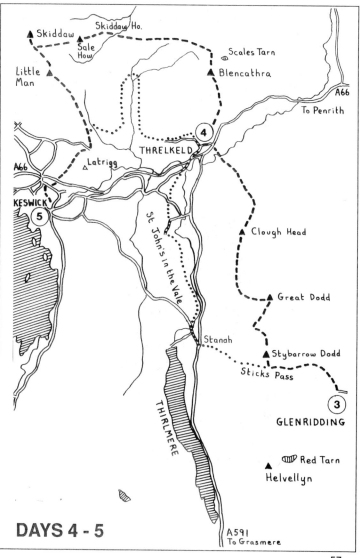

DAYS 4 - 5

Clough Head from St John's in the Vale

DAY 4 GLENRIDDING TO THRELKELD

HIGH LEVEL ROUTE	Distance 8½ miles	Ascent 2,500ft
LOW LEVEL ROUTE	Distance 8½ miles	Ascent 1,800ft

ROUTE SUMMARY

Sticks Pass is the initial objective for both routes which start by climbing to Sticks Hause at 2,500 feet.

High Level Route Turning north from the summit of Sticks Pass the route follows the ridge with easy walking over the grassy and unfrequented Dodds to Clough Head and thence down to the village of Threlkeld.

Low Level Route While Sticks Hause at 2,500 feet is hardly low level, a rapid descent follows to Stanah where there is a youth hostel and this is followed by easy walking through the meadows of St John's in the Vale.

While some speak disparagingly of the "Boring Dodds", these rounded green hills which lie between Sticks Pass and the Northern Fells will appeal to those who delight in the remoter hills, for apart from the sheep, few figures will be seen on their summits and, with easy paths along the ridge, the day's end at Threlkeld is reached surprisingly quickly. This is the longest and most continuously elevated ridge in the whole of the Lake District, stretching for ten miles from High Pike in the south to Clough Head in the north, only once dipping below the 2,000 foot contour, and that for a mere matter of yards at Grisedale Tarn. After a day on Fairfield and another on Helvellyn, this is the barrier that must again be surmounted to reach Threlkeld. Both High and Low Routes start by climbing Sticks Pass, an old pony route, which at nearly 2,500 foot is the highest pass in the Lake District. Originally marked by sticks it was used until 1824 by packhorses carrying the ore from Greenside Mine above Glenridding to the smelting furnace at Stonycroft near Keswick.

From the tops these fells appear to be merely high sheep walks and the presence of steep rock is entirely unsuspected, but low on the western side overlooking St John's in the Vale, the slopes steepen into cliffs. Here is Castle Rock where the spectacular, overhanging front face has yielded some extremely hard climbs.

William Hutchinson, whose book *An Excursion to the Lakes* predated Wordsworth's guide by sixty years, was romantically impressed by Castle Rock:

In the widest part of the dale you are struck with the appearance of an ancient ruined castle, which seems to stand upon the summit of a little mount, the mountains around forming an amphitheatre. This massive bulwark shews a front of various towers, and makes an awful, rude, and gothic appearance with its lofty turrets, and ragged battlements.

In 1813 Sir Walter Scott used Castle Rock as a setting for his poem *The Bridal of Triermain* in which the knight, Sir Roland, storms the enchanted castle in search of the daughter of King Arthur and the Fairy Queen:

> *midmost of the vale, a mound*
> *Arose, with airy turrets crowned,*
> *Buttress, and rampires circling bound,*
> *And mighty keep and tower.*

It has also been linked wih the medieval poem *Sir Gawayne and the Green Knight*. But now the romantic period is over, Castle Rock is no longer regarded with a mixture of awe and wonder, and passing motorists speeding down the busy A591 barely give it a second glance.

St John's in the Vale is thought to take its name from the Knights of St John of Jerusalem who supposedly built a church here in the thirteenth century. The present church, which was built in 1845, replaced a much earlier chapel. In medieval times the main route from Kendal to Keswick passed through the valley where it crossed another important road linking with the Naddle valley on a continuation of the old coach road from Penrith

St John's in the Vale Church

below Clough Head. Nowadays the main road goes the far side of High Rigg where, for a brief moment of glory, it acquires the status of a dual carriageway. The valley of St John's Beck is little frequented by either cars or walkers, but the church remains, isolated in the middle of nowhere with only the Carlisle Diocesan Youth Centre for company.

The old school at Stanah is now Thirlmere Youth Hostel. Nearby Thirlmere was at one time two lakes crossed in the middle by a bridge on stone piers, but in 1894 the water level was raised by 54 feet and the main road was diverted round the newly formed reservoir. It took ten years to build the dam and an aqueduct 96 miles long was constructed to supply thirsty Manchester. From 1910 to 1925 two thousand acres of trees were planted around the reservoir to prevent soil erosion and silting, but as no purification plant was provided the lake was enclosed and the public was barred. However in 1982 a treatment works was built and visitors are now encouraged to follow forest trails and walk along the shore which has recently been opened up.

The snow was falling steadily as we climbed the eastern slopes of Stybarrow Dodd from Dowthwaite, the tiny hamlet which is said to have the fewest hours of sunshine in the Lake District. Several inches of snow lay on the ground and piled in drifts against the grey stone walls. The mist hung low over the tops and as we climbed into it, the sky and ground merged into a world of white. As we climbed higher the snow stopped falling, but the wind increased, driving the snow before us as we struggled along the ridge. It was a wild day and we saw little of the fell or of Watson's Dodd or Great Dodd as we followed a careful compass course over the tops. Then, as we came down the westward slopes of Great Dodd, we broke free of the cloud and a momentary gleam of sunshine turned the white to silver. It was our twenty-fifth wedding anniversary.

JOINT ROUTE

If the night was spent in Glenridding then take the Low Level Route, given on Day 3, to the youth hostel.

From **Helvellyn Youth Hostel** continue past the buildings of the old Greenside Mine and take the unsurfaced track of **Sticks Pass** which zigzags up the hillside by the grassed-over spoil heaps through the dark green bushes of juniper. After a climb of about 500 feet and nearing the top of the first steep ascent, leave the rough road, which is heading for the ski huts, and follow the old way towards Swart Beck. Nearby is the site of the first crushing mill at Greenside which was built in 1834 though later crushing mills were constructed lower down the valley. Crossing the footbridge, the path leads through a dry, sandy, barren waste of spoil heaps where nature is only slowly re-establishing a toehold with occasional small patches of purple thyme. The path then skirts round to the right of the now dry bed of Top Dam which

61

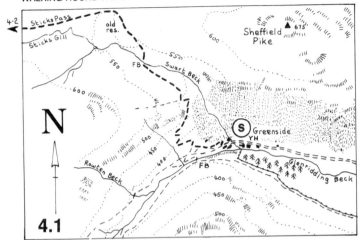

supplied the mine with water power. The earliest levels of the lead mine, the High Horse Levels dating from 1790, were to the right towards the end of the reservoir.

Climbing up and out of the head of the valley high above Sticks Gill, to the left on the slopes of Raise are the pointed roofs of two ski huts. This side of the Helvellyn range holds the snow much longer and a ski tow is available for those who don't mind the long walk, but there seems to have been remarkably little snow in recent years, the warmer winters coinciding with our purchase of cross country skis.

The summit of Sticks Pass is at 2,450 feet, but the ascent is enclosed and protected by the valley sides and there is little exposure to the elements until **Sticks Hause** is reached where the High and Low Level Routes part company.

HIGH LEVEL ROUTE

At the top of Sticks Pass, turn north on the clear path which climbs steeply to the first summit. The rest of the day is kind to the feet as it is softly grassy for the next 6 miles, all the way from here to Threlkeld. At a small cairn on the southern end of **Stybarrow Dodd** the ridge flattens out to give an extensive panorama. Eastwards is the head of Ullswater with Rampsgill Head and High Street beyond and southwards on the far side of Raise is Helvellyn. To the north, Skiddaw and Blencathra appear between the next two Dodds while to the left of Skiddaw the pointed top is yet another Dodd, the low tree-covered fell which overlooks Bassenthwaite. The path bypasses the true summit,

62

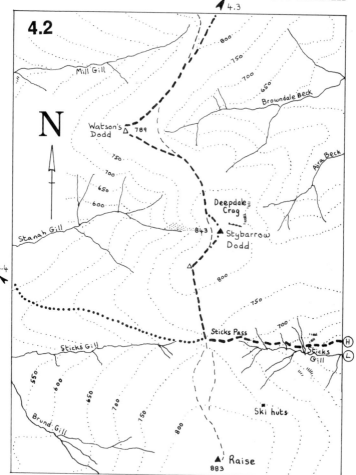

which is a short distance away north-east over pathless short turf, where a small cairn near a section of ruined wall confirms your position.

The summit of Great Dodd looks a long way ahead across the valley of Browndale Beck, but there is little unnecessary loss of height as the ridge kinks north-west sweeping round the steep grassy combe high above Stanah Gill. A path to the right cuts off the corner, but don't miss **Watson's**

Calfhow Pike

Dodd as the ascent is negligible and taking a few steps to the left of the neat little cairn on the grassy top gives a lovely view of Thirlmere, St John's in the Vale and Keswick.

The path continues along the ridge with an easy ascent to the horseshoe-shaped wind shelter on **Great Dodd**, whose orange-coloured summit cairn is a few pathless yards further north. Beyond there is a wide expanse of low-lying land and you feel on the edge of Lakeland as you look down on the end of Ullswater, while on the eastern skyline nearly 25 miles away are the three tops of Cross Fell, Little Dun Fell and Great Dun Fell. On the horizon immediately above the triangular shape of the central piece of Ullswater is Mickle Fell, while closer at hand are the small isolated hills of Great Mell Fell and Little Mell Fell. To the north-west can be glimpsed the end of Derwent Water while to the north beyond Clough Head, the final summit of the day, is the long ridge of Blencathra.

The continuation to Clough Head can be very confusing in mist as the wide grassy ridge makes a semi-circular sweep south-westwards before curving round to the north. Initially there is no path but soon one materialises to the miniature rocky peak of **Calfhow Pike** where the end of Thirlmere is just in view.

It is a grassy dip and an easy pull up of only 300 foot on a clear path to

64

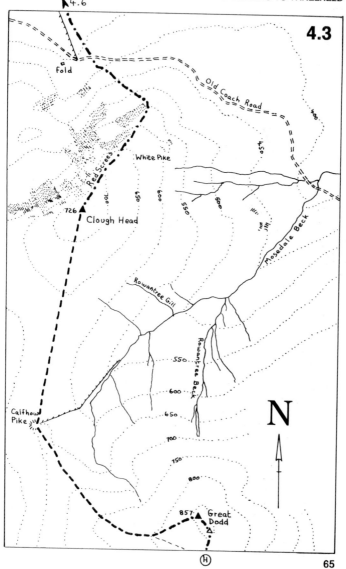

4.6

Fold

Old Coach Road

4.3

400

White Pike

450

Red Screes

700

650

600

550

600

726 ▲ Clough Head

Mosedale Beck

Rowantree Gill

550

Rowantree Beck

600

650

Calfhow Pike

700

N

750

800

857 ▲ Great Dodd
△

Ⓗ

Clough Head, whose summit has a stone OS trig point and a wind shelter. Across the valley is tomorrow's route up Hall's Fell, the best of Blencathra's five southern ridges. To the north-west the scarp slope of Lonscale Fell appears quite strikingly in silhouette, and the broad path visible even at this distance is the popular route from Keswick to Skiddaw summit. To the west is Derwent Water with Grisedale Pike and the North-Western Fells beyond. Causey Pike, identified by the little bump on the end of the ridge, runs up towards Grasmoor in the distance and on the far side of Bassenthwaite Lake the lower fells are almost completely covered in trees.

Follow the ridge north-east, first to a little cairn on the brink of Red Screes and then downhill keeping to the left of White Pike. It is an easy, but pathless descent on grass all the way, curving gently round to the left to descend steeply to cross the fence at a stile onto the **Old Coach Road**. This now quiet track was once the main route from Penrith to Keswick and in the distance the roar of traffic on the A66 is but a murmur as you continue downhill. An old railway carriage perches incongruously on the moor and close by, but hidden in the grass, are the hut circles and ancient walls of a Celtic settlement, an early British village. Descend to the right of the disused Threlkeld Quarry where granite, an extrusion at the junction of the Borrowdale Volcanics and Skiddaw Slates, provided the masonry for the Penrith to Keswick railway around 1862. Later this local stone was used in the construction of Thirlmere Reservoir and, before closing in 1980, road stone was quarried here. A tarmac lane is joined to the left of Newsham cottage which was once known as Tippot Hill. There has been a dwelling here since the middle of the seventeenth century and probably even before that. The lane crosses the disused railway line and the River Glenderamackin to the busy A66. Taking your life in your hands, cross the road to the footpath opposite which enters **Threlkeld** by the back door to emerge conveniently at the rear of the Salutation Inn in the centre of the village.

LOW LEVEL ROUTE

Crossing **Sticks Hause** continue down the western side where the stream, Sticks Gill, which rises at a handy spring has uniquely, but rather confusingly, the same name as the one on the east. Thirlmere now comes into view ahead as the good path crosses a spur to drop into the end of the huge grassy bowl of Stanah Gill with Watson's Dodd and Stybarrow Dodd forming the skyline. At a sheepfold the grassy slopes steepen in more rugged and grand surroundings to descend a grassy rib of ground high above the delightful Stanah Gill with its little falls and pools. Below is Thirlmere with the hamlet of Stanah set back from the busy A591 where cars hurtle along the dual carriageway towards Keswick and the northern Lakes. To the right you can see the back of Castle Rock, though from this angle the imagination is stretched to see any resemblance to a castle.

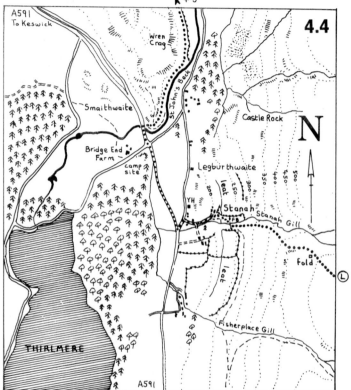

At the intake wall the path bends right to cross the gill at a bridge before descending again through a little gate and a field to the leat dutifully conveying water on behalf of Manchester. Another field, which was occupied by a friendly Thelwell pony on our last visit, is left by a ladder stile to join the lane into **Stanah** where thirsty walkers look in vain for afternoon teas. There is only a scattering of houses, Thirlmere Youth Hostel and a telephone box, while the nearest pub, the King's Head at Thirlspot, is half a mile up the main road in the wrong direction!

Resolutely turning the other way we were overtaken by walkers on the 'Four Peaks Marathon' and were tempted to call at their refreshment stop in the stone-built bus shelter. There is only a quarter of a mile of tarmac with a providentially wide grassy verge, before reaching St John's Beck where the

67

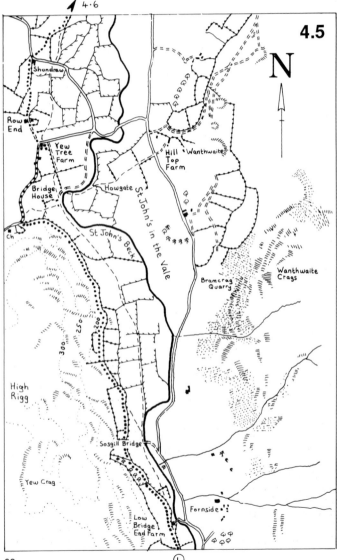

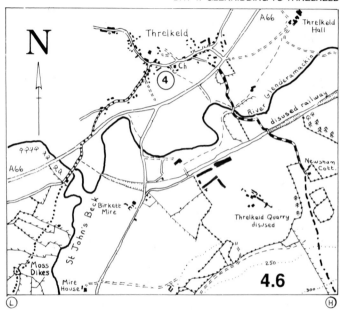

modern bridge has been built on top of the old one which can be seen by peering over the parapet. A ladder stile on the right signed 'St John's in the Vale Church' then leads once more to peace and quiet.

Take the higher path of the two, but don't continue up the fell, and instead contour round the hillside through the trees above the beck. Across the valley, in complete contrast to their upper grassy reaches, the lower slopes of the Dodds are steep, rough and rugged, with Castle Rock on whose overhanging face the easiest route is graded Very Severe. The path follows the beck below the aptly named Wren Crag, where we have seen several of these tiny birds, then passes above Low Bridge End Farm where some new trees including hardwoods have been planted. To the right is the single-span arch of Sosgill Bridge and the path, colourful with speedwells and buttercups, tormentil and lady's mantle, hugs the wall climbing gently with pastoral views of **St John's in the Vale**. Castle Rock now assumes more fortress-like proportions and after a final ascent a lane is joined at a stile by the churchyard where John Richardson, the Cumbrian dialect poem writer, was buried in 1866. He was a mason and helped to build the parsonage and school at St John's in the Vale and also rebuilt the church; later he was the schoolmaster for twenty-two years. The Carlisle Diocesan Youth Centre, which was

69

formed in 1951 from the church school, stands next to the church.

The unfenced lane descends past a tiny one-up, one-down cottage by a gate, then at a bend by Yew Tree Farm, take the footpath to Row End. Passing the cottage, cross the fields towards Blencathra with ahead tomorrow's High Level Route up Hall's Fell. Climbing a small flight of steps the path leads to Shundraw Farm. On the opposite side of the lane a barely trodden path to Threlkeld goes over stiles and through a series of smart new gates for nearly a mile to emerge onto a little lane. Crossing the River Glenderamackin, the track of the abandoned railway and the main A66, the most hazardous exploit of the day, take the minor road for the last quarter mile up into the village of **Threlkeld**.

THRELKELD

The village of Threlkeld has, since the construction of the bypass, become a quiet backwater and though there are no obvious attractions for the visitor it makes a pleasant place to stay. Dominated by the vast bulk of Blencathra which towers over the houses, the village is large enough to boast two pubs, a post office and a school. Originally it was a mining village and after the last lead mine closed in 1910, local men were employed at the Threlkeld Granite Quarry just the other side of the main road, but now that too is closed. Nowadays most of the population work further afield in Keswick or Penrith, though some of the houses are holiday homes.

In Threlkeld there is one of the nicest bed and breakfast places we have found, an old low-beamed cottage with views across to Clough Head. It also has a surprise for visitors. The bathroom door does not have a lock, instead there is a pokerwork sign which may be reversed to indicate occupation. But frequently visitors ducking their heads to avoid the low beams overlook the sign, so opening the door is always an interesting event.

The name Threlkeld comes from the Norse and means the 'Spring of the Serf' from 'kelda' meaning 'spring' and 'thrall' describing the local inhabitants; it has been known as this for at least 800 years. The first settlement was on the slopes of Clough Head around 300 to 900 AD and would have been a clearing in the densely wooded countryside. After the coming of the Norsemen the site of the present village was occupied and by 1220 Threlkeld had a priest named Randulph and also presumably a church. The present church of Saint Mary's was built in 1777 on the same site as previous churches. The tiles on the floor were made at Threlkeld Quarry and the font is of Threlkeld granite.

From 1864 the village was served by the Cockermouth, Keswick and Penrith Railway which carried both minerals and passengers, but after the advent of British Rail the railway was unable to compete with road transport and the service declined before finally closing in 1972. The old route through Threlkeld from Penrith to Keswick was improved in 1745 by making it into a turnpike road. It was then rebuilt by Mr McAdam in 1824 and lastly the A66 by-pass was built in 1965.

The building marked as the sanatorium on old maps is a mile or so from the village and is passed by tomorrow's Low Level Route. Standing alone on the 1,000-foot contour it was built in 1904 as an isolation hospital for sufferers from tuberculosis. Before the discovery of sulphonamides there was no cure for the disease other than rest and fresh air and this privately funded hospital was only the second sanatorium to open in England. When, because of new drugs and immunisation of the population against TB, the building was no longer needed for its original use, it became a geriatric hospital, finally closing in 1975. It is now the Blencathra Centre and offers family and group accommodation for holidays in a beautiful setting.

Celandines

Skiddaw and Derwent Water from Surprise View

DAY 5 THRELKELD TO KESWICK

HIGH LEVEL ROUTE	Distance 12 miles	Ascent 4,350ft
LOW LEVEL ROUTE	Distance 8 miles	Ascent 950ft

ROUTE SUMMARY

High Level Route This gives an energetic day climbing two grand mountains. Blencathra is reached via Narrow Edge, an exhilarating scramble up a rocky ridge and this is followed by a pathless grassy descent to the wild country Back o'Skiddaw and the remote Skiddaw House. Skiddaw is climbed from the back, an easy ascent over the minor summit of Sale How then the descent to Keswick is on good paths all the way.

Low Level Route Contouring high above the valley round the lower slopes of the fells, the route can be extended to include either Blencathra or Skiddaw.

NOTE: It is possible to change from one route to the other at the half-way point.

Unlike many of the Lake District mountains whose best is hidden from sight beyond the valley head and only appreciated after a long approach, Blencathra and Skiddaw show their finest sides to the south where the race track of the A66 passes the very foot of their slopes.

These hills are of slate, a crumbly, flaky sort rather than the lovely green and blue slabs of which so many houses and cottages are built, but it is old. These are the oldest rocks in the Lake District, formed 500 million years ago as sediments in a primeval sea in which dwelt tiny creatures, graptolites and trilobites whose remains can be seen as an occasional white streak in the rocks or the shaly debris of the paths.

The lowest of the Lake District three-thousanders, Skiddaw is massive, its long summit ridge of bare grey rocks and stones flanked on either hand by steep slopes of grey scree and fronted by a subsidiary range of hills which rise in a long undulating ridge to join the mountain's southern slopes. Blencathra, however, faces straight onto the road, with no less than five great buttresses of grass, heather and rock rising to its long, but mainly grassy summit ridge. John Ruskin, the writer, artist and critic, inspired by the Hall's Fell approach to Blencathra up the rocky crest of Narrow Edge, wrote:

It is the finest thing I've yet seen, there being several bits of real crag-work and a fine view at the top over the great plain of Penrith on one side, and the Cumberland hills, as a chain, on the other.

While the majority of the Lake District's ice-scoured combes face north-east, on the lee side of the mountain where the bulk of the snow was deposited during the Ice Age, many of Blencathra's combes, which divide one buttress from the next, face south. No doubt experts puzzle over why this should be so, but this means that the most interesting ways to reach Blencathra are all on the side which is easy to approach.

Although the Ice Age finally came to an end around ten thousand years ago, ice continues, every winter, to alter the mountains, prising off pieces of rock to join the scree at the foot of the cliffs. The effects of the winter freeze can also be seen on flat or gently sloping ground on some mountain summits where stones appear in strange geometrical patterns on the ground. This is best seen on the slopes of Skiddaw Little Man where narrow parallel lines of bare earth look at first glance like sheep trods. Repeated freeze and thaw causes small stones to come to the surface and the constant movement prevents vegetation getting a hold. Parallel lines tend to form at right angles to a slope, while on flatter areas, such as the summit of Skiddaw, the stones form patches of bare ground.

Skiddaw and Blencathra are the giants of the northern hills, on view to all, forming the northern skyline and apparently the northern edge of the Lake District. But when their summits are reached the hills beyond come into sight. This is Back o'Skiddaw, a wild bleak country with more affinity for the Pennines perhaps than the Lakeland fells, but a beautiful quiet area of heather-clad hills where you can still walk for hours without seeing another figure in the landscape.

The moorland Back o'Skiddaw is now grazed only by sheep, but until the 1950s the land to the west was managed as a grouse moor. To the east, on the Blencathra side, the land is grass, where Swaledale and Rough Fell flocks roam the hills, but westwards are the heather-clad fellsides of Great Calva, Knott and Great Sca Fell. While at one time regular burning of the heather prompted new growth whose fresh tips were food for the grouse, now that active management of the moor has ceased the heather is growing lank and straggly providing the birds with little cover or food. In time the incessant nibbling of the sheep will render the moor indistinguishable from the eastern part which has been sheepwalk much longer.

It is fragile country and once the surface vegetation has been stripped away the underlying peat quickly becomes an oozing black morass, but fortunately there are few paths, save the track to Skiddaw House. This is the only habitation Back o'Skiddaw. Originally a row of shepherds' cottages, the last shepherd retired in 1969 and after a period as a school outdoor pursuits centre, it was renovated and became a youth hostel. However, as no planning permission was obtained the hostel was forced to close and its future was in doubt until permission was given for use as a bothy on appeal. The sheepfolds on these hills, unlike those of most of the Lake District, are

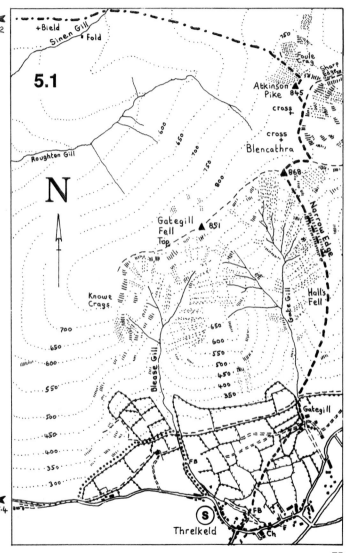

often circular in shape, recalling those on the Cheviot which were reputedly invented by George Napier, one of Nelson's captains.

While grouse and sheep divided these hills between them, the northern side of the fells was once a major mining area for copper, zinc, manganese, and several other metals including silver; there was even a china clay mine. At its peak in the mid-nineteenth century, around 1,500 tons of copper ore a year were extracted from the Roughtongill Mine, the most productive of these mines; this was equivalent to about half the output from Coniston. Roughtongill to the north is remote and difficult to reach, but just above Threlkeld, on the slopes of Blencathra at the foot of the Hall's Fell ridge, is the Gategill Mine which was in production even before the introduction of gunpowder. The rock was split using the old tools of 'stope and feather'. A hole was drilled in the rock and two strips of iron inserted, round on one side and flat on the other. The stope, a thin wedge, was then hammered in between and so split the rock. Threlkeld prospered for a time with around 100 men employed in the mines, but like so many in the Lake District, the mine's success was brief and the village is now a peaceful place.

ROUTE DESCRIPTION

HIGH LEVEL ROUTE
From the end of Blease Road in the centre of **Threlkeld** a track, signed Public Footpath, leads past some houses and forks right over a footbridge. Climbing straight towards Hall's Fell a series of new stiles leads across the fields to join the track coming up from Threlkeld by Gategill Farm. Below are the kennels of the Blencathra Foxhounds which were established in 1840, and the buildings and spoil tips of the old Threlkeld mine. This mine, which dates from the seventeenth century, was a big lead and zinc mine and very productive until its closure in 1928. A signpost points the way between the farm buildings to a kissing gate on the left of Gate Gill with its little falls. Climb to a second gate by a seat, thoughtfully placed there by the Friends of the Lake District, and out onto the open fellside.

Crossing Gate Gill take the little path which, after a steep start, zigzags its way up grassy slopes. Higher up the vegetation changes to heather and the path climbs to reach the rocky ridge of **Narrow Edge**. The rocks are interesting, but not difficult and the path scrambles over and around them to emerge onto Hallsfell Top, the very highest point of **Blencathra**.

To the south-west the summit ridge runs out to the subsidiary top of Gategill Fell, beyond is the silver sheen of Derwent Water and further still are the high Western Fells, Scafell Pike, Gable and Pillar. There is no cairn, only a few stones scraped together, but after the rocky edge of the ascent the view ahead is dramatically different. To the west is Skiddaw, its northern grassy slopes sweeping down to the few lonely trees that hide Skiddaw House, but

Atkinson Pike, Blencathra

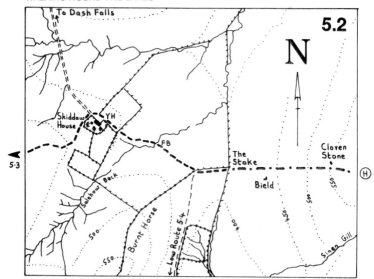

this is the only dwelling and into the distance stretches open grassland and heather moor with a far skyline of unfrequented hills.

Although the next objective is Skiddaw, the descent from Blencathra lies at first in almost the opposite direction leading north to Atkinson Pike, another of Blencathra's summits. Following the path round the edge, taking care not to descend inadvertently to Scales Fell, Scales Tarn briefly comes into view beneath Sharp Edge before you veer left passing a white cross of stones to the cairn on the summit of **Atkinson Pike**. The cross was constructed by Harold Robinson of Threlkeld to commemorate the death of a walker and another smaller cross can be seen just below Blencathra's summit.

A few steps to the north a small cairn marks the start of the zigzag route down through the screes above Foule Crag. When the stones give way to grass, by a little knoll from which there is a good view of Sharp Edge, turn left and strike westwards towards Skiddaw House over pathless but easy grassy slopes. Rounding the head of Roughten Gill and then Sinen Gill it is a wild open moor with few landmarks save the distant hills. A bield is passed hidden among the rushes on the way to the elusive Cloven Stone. This boundary stone, were it situated anywhere else in the Lakes would surely pass both unnoticed and unnamed.

Continue westwards, aiming to the left of Skiddaw House and descend

Skiddaw House

on grass between the stones to cross the only piece of dry ground hereabouts to **The Stake**, another boundary stone sitting in a large boggy puddle. Follow the fence across to the Cumbria Way. Turn right for Skiddaw House.

The Low Level Route to Keswick may be joined here, omitting Skiddaw, by turning left to follow the path above Glenderaterra Beck.

The track crosses a rather shabby heather moor and after a footbridge over Salehow Beck climbs to **Skiddaw House** with its cape of larch trees. The track passes in front of the house whose windows look out on the wide and open landscape Back o'Skiddaw, then rounding the corner of the wood a small path climbs westwards becoming an obvious track which leads through the grass and moth-eaten heather to the top of **Sale How**. This grassy lump on the lower slopes of Skiddaw has a small cairn on its top which is visited more frequently than its lack of obvious attractions would suggest, as this counts as a separate 2,000 foot top.

Dipping to the col beyond, the grassy path continues up the slope to the spine of Skiddaw, but fades out just before the main track is reached. Turn right to a stile and gate through the fence and the broad stony highway climbs easily to the long, almost level, summit ridge of **Skiddaw**.

A few patches of grass cling tenaciously and in summer even crimson cowberries can be found, but all else is a barren waste of scree. The highest point is at the far northern end, where an OS trig point, a windshelter and a topograph commemorating the Silver Jubilee of Queen Elizabeth II, crowd together on the highest, coldest and windiest spot. To the south the high western hills form the skyline and far below to the west are the white sails of boats on Bassenthwaite Lake. This is strangely the only 'lake' in the Lake District, all the others being 'meres' or 'waters'. Immediately after the Ice Age,

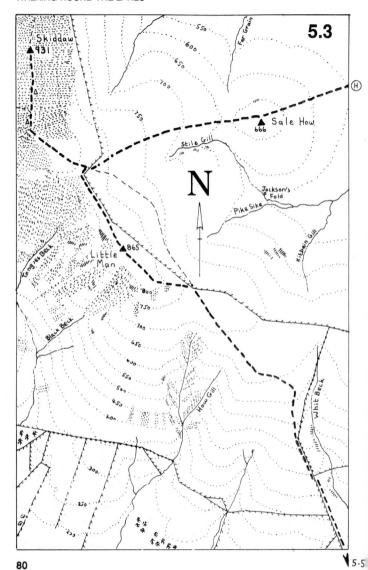

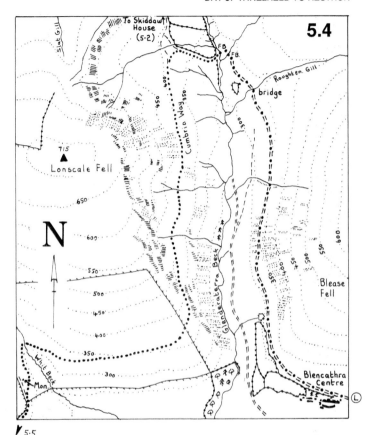

when glaciers scooped out the hollows, the lake was joined to Derwent Water forming one large sheet of water, but the River Greta, the "rocky river", brought down rocks and silt which eventually separated the two.

Retrace your steps along the ridge and down to the fence where the parallel stripes on the slopes of **Skiddaw Little Man** are caused by frost heaving. Weather permitting, Keswick and Derwent Water are seen spread out below and strong walkers will want to include Skiddaw Little Man by following the fence rightwards to the summit. Lesser mortals should stay on the main path which curves round to the left of the Little Man high above the grassy bowl of Pike Sike. Crossing the fence again, the path descends gradually with occasional stones speckled white with tiny fossils. These are graptolites, 500 million years old and among the earliest creatures on earth. The path then bends right to drop steeply down above the ravine of Whit Beck and after crossing a stile to the other side of the fence, continues descending to a little col. On a recent visit this slope was busy with novice paragliders being tutored in the art of throwing themselves off a mountain. Multicoloured parachutes in pink and yellow lay scattered about and as we watched, another aspirant hauled his canopy into the air and sailed up into the sky.

From the col the path climbs briefly to the **Shepherd's Monument** where the Low Route is joined.

LOW LEVEL ROUTE

From the centre of **Threlkeld** take 'Blease Road leading to Blencathra' and at the bend turn off up the grassy lane signed 'Blease and Blencathra'. The track dips into a little wooded clough to cross the stream at a footbridge, then climbs a flight of steps and out to a gate onto the open fellside. Turning left across Blease Gill, a permissive footpath follows the wall round to a lane. This is a more attractive route than the right of way which passes through the fields above the farms. To the left you can see the full length of St John's in the Vale with Castle Rock rising up in the centre below Helvellyn Lower Man.

The public bridleway to Skiddaw House runs along the grass verge of the lane past the **Blencathra Centre**. This old sanatorium was purchased by the Lake District Special Planning Board in 1976 and now offers self catering accommodation to individuals and groups. At the end of the lane the track then swings up the valley of the Glenderaterra Beck between Blease Fell and Lonscale Fell. After climbing gently the track crosses a gill then descends equally gently to a broad clapper bridge over Roughten Gill. In the valley below was the Brundholme mine, a small lead mine which was worked in the nineteenth century. Copper and barytes were also found, but mining ceased around 1880. A little further down the valley is the earlier Blencathra mine. At the head of the valley after crossing two little footbridges and a ladder stile, follow the wall up and then turn left climbing to join the **Cumbria Way**.

The High Level Route to Skiddaw House may be joined here by turning right to follow the wall towards Skiddaw House.

The Cumbria Way climbs very gently for half a mile. To the left you can just pick out the insignificant bump of the Cloven Stone on the skyline and above on the right is the rocky crest of Lonscale Fell. The path then descends gradually beneath steep craggy slopes along a little rocky terrace high above the valley. Rounding the corner to a gate and a stile across a fence, Latrigg appears ahead and the broad grassy track continues down to a hairpin bend across Whit Beck. A short ascent then brings you to a gate beyond the **Shepherd's Monument** where the returning High Level Route is joined.

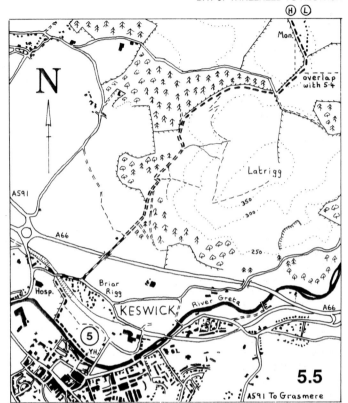

JOINT ROUTE

From the monument *In loving memory of two Skiddaw shepherds* who were noted breeders of prize Herdwick sheep, take the broad path to the left of the fence through the kissing gate and out to the lane end. Turn right and then left on the bridleway beside the wood. The summit of **Latrigg**, whose name derives from the Norse for Open Field, is only a ten-minute dash up the grassy slopes and the climb is well worth the effort for the fine views down into Borrowdale, a taste of the joys to come.

The broad path hugs the edge of the wood then zigzags through an open area to another wood. After passing down a gorse-covered hillside below a larch plantation with wide views to the right of the North-Western Fells, the

83

track joins the end of Spooney Green Lane by a house. Crossing the A66, the Keswick bypass, at a new bridge, the unsurfaced lane reaches the road and new houses of Briar Rigg. Turn right and then left through a gate by the disused railway line to follow a tarmac path along the edge of a field and into **Keswick** Park. Taking the tarmac path beside the River Greta, Keswick Youth Hostel, a former hotel, is reached via the bridge at the far end of the park.

KESWICK

Busy with visitors throughout the season, the little Victorian town of Keswick makes a good centre from which to explore the northern Lakes. Originally a mining town, it expanded hugely in the second half of the nineteenth century with the coming of the railway and the tourists in 1864.

There is plenty here for a wet day's amusement. Outdoor pursuits shops abound alongside the ubiquitous gift shops. There are numerous pubs, several bookshops and even a Woolworths which stocks boots and water-proofs. The cake shop is excellent and there are some equally good food stores. In the old-fashioned Fitzpark Museum on the edge of the park there is a scale model of the Lake District which Wordsworth examined in 1840 and greatly approved of, mentioning it in the forword of the fourth edition of his *Guide to the Lakes*. There is also a 500-year-old cat, many geological specimens, a stone xylophone and some original manuscripts of the Lake Poets. The more modern Cumberland Pencil Museum is also well worth a visit.

If the clouds break, a stroll down to Derwent Water past the clock golf and the Century Theatre is a must. The theatre was a mobile one from 1952 to 1975 but there are plans to replace it with a permanent building. There are boats for hire or you can walk to Friar's Crag which was 'The Peak of Darien' in Arthur Ransome's *Swallows and Amazons.*

> *Roger climbed up through the trees to the top of the promontory. At last he came out of the trees on a small open space of bare rock and heather. This was the Peak of Darien. There were trees all round it, but through them could be seen the bright glimmer of the lake.*

Every night from Easter to October there is something going on in Keswick. The Moot Hall, whose ground floor arches were originally used as market stalls, is now an information centre and often has a slide show in the upstairs room. There may be an illustrated lecture in one of the many other halls in the town or you could visit the little cinema. Some days you will be spoilt with a choice of entertainment. We spent one October half term here and were out every evening!

They breed 'em tough in Keswick. Looking one evening for the school where the lecture was to be held we asked the way of an elderly lady. "That's where I'm going," she said, as we quickened our pace to follow her. "I'm sorry
84

I'm a bit slow," she added, "I lost my leg in a car accident last year."

We have a soft spot for Keswick. Extending our Easter honeymoon by two nights, we arrived on the bus from Ambleside and after choosing one of the unmemorable but cheap bed and breakfast with which Keswick abounds (there are reputed to be more B & Bs in Keswick than in any town of this size in the country), we discovered a young climber lecturing on "The North Face of the Eiger" in the back room of a pub. Captivated we returned the following evening for a second installment on "The Towers of Paine" and have been fans of Chris Bonington ever since.

The Shepherds' monument

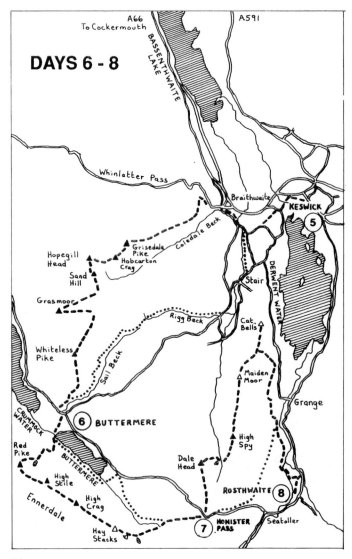

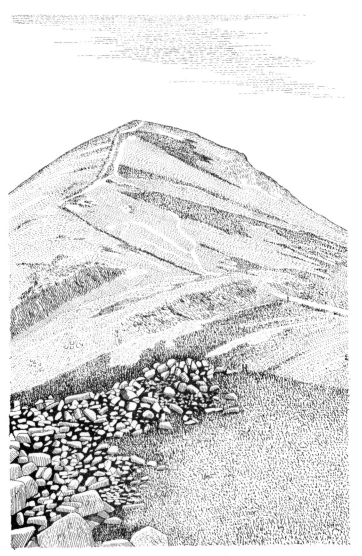

Grisedale Pike, the south-west ridge

| HIGH LEVEL ROUTE | Distance 12 miles | Ascent 3,800ft |
| LOW LEVEL ROUTE | Distance 10 miles | Ascent 1,250ft |

ROUTE SUMMARY

Heading west through Portinscale the High and Low routes divide just before Braithwaite.

High Level Route Climbing to Grisedale Pike by way of the east ridge, the route continues over Hopegill Head and Sand Hill to Grasmoor, the highest of the North-Western Fells, before descending over Whiteless Pike to the little village of Buttermere. The walking is easy on good paths throughout.

Low Level Route Turning south beside Newlands Beck to the hamlet of Stair then, rounding the end of Causey Pike, the route follows Rigg Beck up to a high col at about 1,700 feet where Sail Beck leads down to Buttermere.

Braithwaite was cold and colourless under the gloom of a grey December day. No hint of a breeze stirred the few leaves that still hung on the almost bare branches and on the brown slopes of long dead bracken lay a few patches of grey snow. There were no hills to be seen and in the half light the day seemed ready to end before it had even begun.

We plodded steadily up the road, shoulders complaining under the weight of overfilled rucksacks, and then leaving the tarmac, began the long climb up the east ridge of Grisedale Pike. Frost had been at work on the path, lifting the stones on needles of ice, forming a honeycomb that crunched and crumbled under our feet. Dimly we could see the grey shapes of the bare pines of Whinlatter Forest and on the still air the sound of a saw rose faintly from the valley below. No sound, no voices, no other people; a few footprints marked the snow, but we walked alone.

The ground steepened as Sleet How was reached, then gradually as we climbed the cloud seemed to thin. Above us the grey now had a hint of blue. A faint breath of wind brushed us as the mist drifted past, eddying and swirling as it subsided towards the valley, then suddenly it was gone and we broke through.

Ahead the ridge seemed to rise vertically to Grisedale Pike, above us the sky was cobalt, and all around was the sea. A white sea that rolled in waves and lapped against the mountain and broke in foam along the shore and from the sea rose islands of even more brilliant white lit by the dazzling sun. To the north-east Skiddaw appeared as a great alpine peak with blue-shadowed slopes rising from the sea that filled the vale of Keswick. Eastwards Clough Head marked the headland of the long island on the eastern horizon which stretched into the distance over Helvellyn to the far off Fairfield. South were the Scafells and much closer at hand the ridge from Causey Pike to Grasmoor was a black silhouette against the sun. Watching, we stood there until our faces grew numb with the cold. We turned and climbed on, into the land of ice and snow.

As you look from Keswick across the roofs of the town to Grisedale Pike and the North-Western Fells in winter or early spring, at summits white with snow glistening in the morning sunshine, the scene is almost alpine. Steep slopes climb to high ridges which link the summits and though the area lacks the tarns which are so characteristic of the Lake District, the pattern of ridges radiating like the spokes of a wheel from Coledale Hause forms a Lake District in miniature. To the north is Whinlatter Forest, dating from 1919 and the first Forestry Commission planting in the Lake District to provide pit props for the mining industry, and from these tree-clad lower slopes a long crest climbs to Grisedale Pike.

While it looks so impressive from the Keswick side, Grisedale Pike is not in fact the highest of the North-Western Fells and is overtopped by Grasmoor, at 2,795 feet just two hundred feet higher. But despite the grandeur of its south-western face, which falls in a continuous steep plunge to Crummock Water over 2,000 feet below, Grasmoor's summit is flat and is linked by gentle slopes to Crag Hill on the east.

At the apex of four converging ridges Grisedale Pike must be on the agenda of any fellwalker staying at Keswick and its ascent proves much easier than expected. With good paths throughout, the miles pass easily on these fells and it is tempting to see how many can be climbed in a day. After one such energetic summer's day climbing all the two-thousanders between Whinlatter and Newlands we came back to Braithwaite in the fading light to see a deer quietly browsing in the forest.

Although these fells belong to the Skiddaw Slates rather than the rough and rugged Borrowdale Volcanics, they are no rounded grassy mounds but steep mountain-shaped mountains with rocks and cliffs. The rock may be broken and unfit for climbers, but these are still excellent crags among some of the finest hills in Lakeland.

Beneath Grisedale Pike at the head of the two-mile long valley of Coledale Beck is the last working mine in the Lake District. The Force Crag mine was initially a lead mine, but from the 1860s to the 1880s barytes was mined here, which was used for polishing glass at St Helens. In 1912 it was reopened by the Coledale Mining Syndicate which worked it on and off until 1947 when the mine was flooded and then in the 1960s the mine was again examined for new veins. The mine is at two levels. The higher workings are

Suspension bridge at Portinscale

the most recent, but it was difficult to remove the ore from these and in 1950 an aerial ropeway was replaced by an underground inclined tunnel from the lower workings. In 1990 it was the only mine still working in the Lake District National Park and was being mined for zinc using compressed air drills which produce a slurry by incorporating water. This has eliminated problems such as silicosis which was caused by the miners inhaling dust. Force Crag Mine only employs four people, but it is producing as much ore in one hour as twenty to thirty men once did in a full day's work.

The eastern slopes of Grasmoor were already in the evening shadows as we collected water from the spring feeding Gasgale Gill. Icicles rimmed the stream and patches of snow crunched beneath our boots as the temperature fell and night approached. The fell tops were still lit by an orange glow and we hurried to reach the crest just in time to see the orange disc of the sun sinking into the Solway Firth. We pitched the tent a few yards from the cairn and then, reluctant to end the day, sat beside the stones watching

90

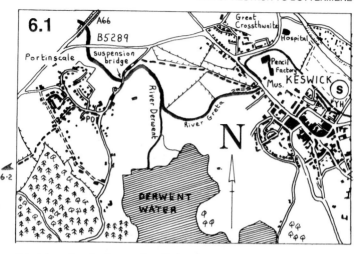

the dying glow in the west until the stars came out and the lights of Whitehaven shone in the darkness.

ROUTE DESCRIPTION

JOINT ROUTE

Leaving **Keswick** on the Cockermouth road, turn left beside the River Greta just after crossing Greta Bridge. This was rebuilt in 1926 and is opposite the Cumberland pencil factory and museum. The field path signed 'Portinscale' runs behind the houses and to the right rises Skiddaw and its satellites, Dodd Fell, Carl Side and Little Man. On reaching the old road turn left and cross the River Derwent by a bouncy suspension bridge. The original Long Bridge was destroyed by storms in the 1950s and a temporary Bailey Bridge was replaced by this grand footbridge. The River Derwent, which has been lingering in Derwent Water, is now joined by the River Greta, the "rocky river", and together they bustle on to Bassenthwaite Lake and Cockermouth, where the River Cocker swells the flow to Workington and the Irish Sea.

By-passed by the busy A66, **Portinscale** looks eminently respectable, with neat cottages, a hotel or two and a village store, but it must have had a dubious past as the name means the harlot's hut. Keeping to the right through the village turn left just after passing Dorothy Well with its biblical quotation,

Whosoever drinketh of this water shall thirst again, but whosoever drinketh of the water that I shall give him, shall never thirst.

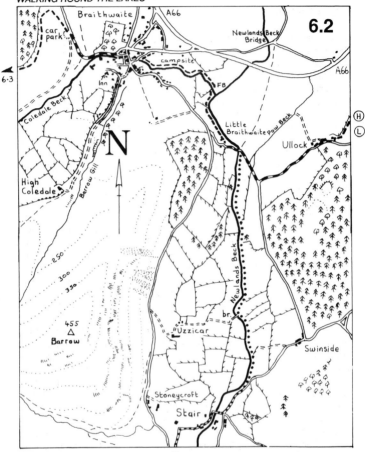

The unsurfaced road is signed 'Footpath to Ullock and Swinside', but it soon becomes a footpath and crossing a lane descends between high hedges to a footbridge, with Causey Pike and Grisedale Pike straight ahead. After crossing the first field to a gate, the blackthorn hedge is followed to emerge onto a narrow lane to the left of Yew Tree Cottage. Turn right through the tiny hamlet of Ullock, then right again in a quarter of a mile at the T-junction towards Braithwaite and along the lane to **Newlands Beck**.

HIGH LEVEL ROUTE

After crossing Newlands Beck take the permissive path to the right through the farm buildings of Little Braithwaite and follow the track beside the beck. A footbridge leads to the other side of Coledale Beck which is then followed upstream on a raised bank over a stile and through a campsite into the village of **Braithwaite**. Turn left and then right to the Whinlatter Pass road. Explorations will reveal two pubs, a cafe and a second-hand bookshop. The Cumberland pencil factory started life here in 1868 but thirty years later the factory was destroyed by fire and it moved to Keswick.

Walk up the pass for 400 yards to a small car park in a gravel pit. Taking the footpath signed 'Grisedale Pike', this rises steeply, first up a flight of steps and then takes a hairpin bend back to climb by the edge of Whinlatter Forest to a stile high above Braithwaite. This section of the forest is called Hospital Plantation after Lakeland View on the Whinlatter Pass which was once a fever hospital. The broad path continues climbing past the forest corner and up the ridge. Briefly the path levels out and dips to a grassy col before the ascent continues up the narrow ridge of Sleet How with views to the right over Whinlatter Forest. A final steep, stony ascent leads to the insignificant cairn on the rocky top of **Grisedale Pike**. This summit and most of the North-Western Fells are formed from the same crumbly rock known as the Skiddaw Slates. This is a fine viewpoint for Skiddaw and the Eastern Fells on the far side of Derwent Water. To the north lie the lower hills of Thornthwaite Forest with the Solway Firth and Scotland beyond, while far to the south are the Scafells and Bow Fell.

Continue along the ridge in a south-westerly direction beside the ruined wall to the summit of **Hobcarton Crag** which has a small cairn on the rocky top. Hobcarton Gill at the foot of the cliffs looks a long way down and although they are of broken rock and of no interest to climbers, here the Skiddaw Slates have a quartz band unusually rich in pyrites where a very rare flower, the red alpine catchfly, can be found. This is one of its only two locations in Britain, the other being in the Scottish Highlands.

The next couple of tops can be omitted by taking the path which short cuts left down to Coledale Hause, but this avoids the edge and the best views. Continue following the edge to the col with its awesome drop over Hobcarton Crag to the right and climb steeply by the edge to the towering peak of **Hopegill Head** which, in spite of its forbidding appearance, is quickly reached. The summit is at the junction of three ridges with the northern one descending over Ladyside Pike towards the Vale of Lorton. Once known as Lady's Seat, it is a fitting companion for Lord's Seat on the other side of Whinlatter Pass and perhaps these names date back to when this area was a hunting forest. The most tempting of the ridges, flanked by Gasgale Crags which fall steeply to Gasgale Gill, is the western one which links the mountain

93

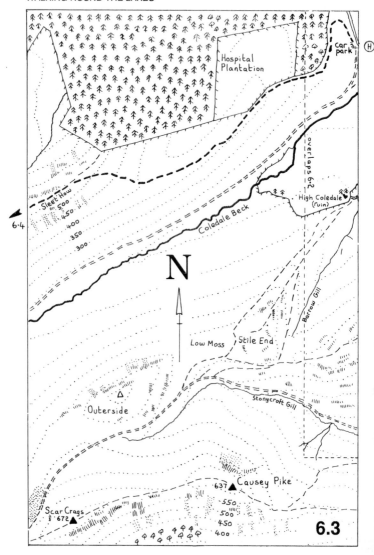

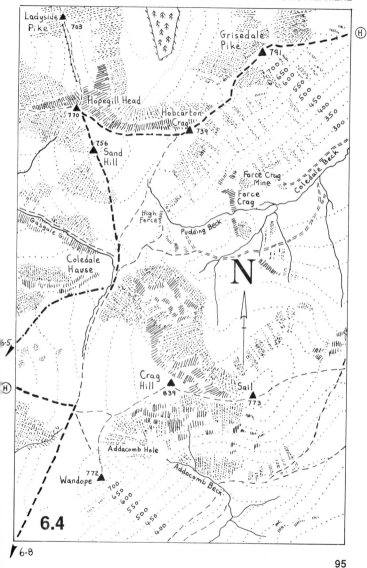

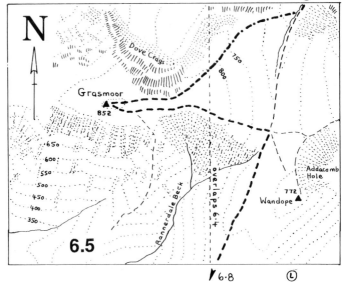

6.5

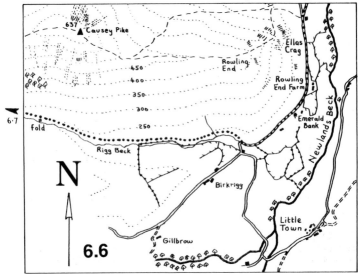

6.6

to Whiteside and beyond is Crummock Water. To the south the bulk of Grasmoor blocks the view, but framed between it and the adjacent Crag Hill are Gable and the Scafells. Further to the east is the easily identifiable thimble-shaped Pike o'Stickle.

Retrace your steps for a few yards towards the col, and then bear right to the cairn on the gently rounded top of **Sand Hill**, which is dwarfed by the surrounding summits. Bare scree slopes lead easily down to **Coledale Hause**, a flat grassy expanse, a complete contrast to the surrounding craggy fells. In medieval times this was part of the Forest of Copeland and there are few stone walls as these fells were preserved as a deer forest. The fenced shafts to the left are old workings of the Force Crag Mine.

Joining the good path beside Gasgale Gill, the summit of **Grasmoor** is a detour which can be avoided by staying on the main path. The highest of these North-Western Fells is visited by crossing the stream near the waterfalls. Taking to the steep grassy slopes follow the ridge westwards, keeping to the edge for the best views where a series of fine gullies drop steeply to the gill. After nearly a mile the summit plateau is reached, an extensive and broad flat ridge with a windshelter marking the highest point at the far end. A few steps further reveal Crummock Water and Buttermere with the highest fells of Lakeland beyond. Opinions differ on the meaning of Grasmoor which may be simply grassy moor or may be derived from the old Norse word 'griss' because pigs were grazed here.

A good path leads east gently downhill and soon the main path is rejoined. Continuing south this rises to a cairn overlooking the screes of Grasmoor which fall steeply to Crummock Water two thousand feet below. Ahead the ridge descends to the cone of Whiteless Pike with Red Pike, tomorrow's objective, beyond across the valley. Above High Crag is Pillar and further left Great Gable rises majestically above the surrounding fells.

Continuing along the narrow rocky edge, a final climb brings you to **Whiteless Pike**. From the small cairn on the flat grassy platform you look down on Buttermere and the neat green fields which separate the lake from Crummock Water. It is thought that towards the end of the Ice Age these two lakes were joined as one.

The path wriggles southwards down the broad ridge to Whiteless Breast then descends south-west past the knobbly end of the Rannerdale Knotts ridge. In medieval times there was a settlement with a chapel in the little valley of Rannerdale, but now all traces of this have disappeared. Veer left above the trees through the rocky knolls to join the wall and the path that leads to the road above **Buttermere** village.

LOW LEVEL ROUTE

Just before **Newlands Beck** turn left on the public footpath to Stair. The path runs beside the beck on a raised bank for a good mile passing a little arched

Whiteless Pike

stone bridge to Uzzicar Farm and the old mine workings. Mining began at Barrow lead mine around 1680, though the spoil heaps by the farm date from about 1883 when there was an enormous sixty-foot water-wheel in use. The mine closed only six years later. Turn right on the lane and then keep right over the bridge and through the hamlet of **Stair**, whose mill was working until 1914. Stair House, dated 1647, is reputed to have been the home of General Fairfax, one of Oliver Cromwell's henchmen.

Turn left at the road junction below Rowling End. By the gill at Stoneycroft is the site of a seventeenth century smelt mill. As well as processing the ore

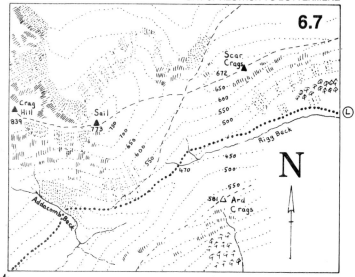

from the local mines, lead from Greenside Mine was brought here by packhorse over Sticks Pass to be smelted.

The tarmac can be avoided by climbing a little up the hillside where a faint path contours the slope. After half a mile leave the road at the sharp bend and take the track climbing to the right of **Rigg Beck**, which soon dwindles to a footpath. On the slopes of Causey Pike above is a natural oak wood, possibly a remnant of the original trees which once covered the Lake District. The stony little path leads to a broad grassy col where Red Pike with the silver ribbon of Sourmilk Gill lies ahead and to the left is the high, almost level ridge of Ard Crags.

As you continue towards Buttermere, Wandope and the huge bowl of Addicombe Hole, a hanging valley, come into view. The little alpine path crosses the deep indentation of Addacombe Beck which tumbles down in waterfalls, then continues high above **Sail Beck,** gradually descending for a couple of miles, dropping down in steps to the track that runs above the fence. On the other side of the valley high above the stream is the road over Newlands Hause.

After passing above a small wood on the banks of Mill Beck, the High Route comes in from the right. Go through a little gate, past the cottages and left down the lane into **Buttermere**.

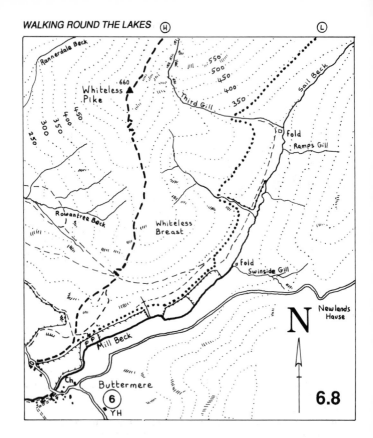

BUTTERMERE

Tiny Buttermere village, dominated by its two inns, stands back from the lake on the edge of the alluvial flats between Buttermere and Crummock Water. The school and the post office are long gone, but there is a youth hostel and Hassness, a Ramblers' Association guest house, and slightly aloof from the village is the small church, built in 1841 on the site of an earlier medieval chapel. Most of the land and the lake is now owned by the National Trust.

Buttermere, gouged out by the glaciers, is deep, going down for nearly one hundred feet at its head and in some lighting conditions it can be a marvellous colour varying from green to blue to blue-grey. There are pike, perch and trout and the deep water fish, the char, which is fished from rowing

100

Buttermere Church

boats using a long, heavily weighted line with bright metal spinners. Potted char was a famous local delicacy, the fish being sold in little pots covered with melted butter.

A full inch of rain had fallen overnight following a very wet day and though we were still dry under our Gortex, we began to steam descending into Buttermere as the sun came out. In the farmyard two small children played in the mud and beside them a few walkers sat on benches with mugs of tea. We eased our packs to the ground and joined them. The tea was good and almost half asleep in the sun we sat and relaxed. The little girl rode her tricycle in the middle of the yard oblivious to the newly arrived car. Her brother was enjoying himself kneeling beside a large brown puddle. He immersed both arms to the elbow, gathering handfuls of mud and dung and squidging them thoughtfully. He rose to his feet and headed in our direction. "If I smack my hands together this is going to go all over you!" he said, and it did.

The Bridge Inn beside Mill Beck was once a corn-mill, while at the end of the eighteenth century the Fish was the home of 'The Maid of Buttermere'. In his *Fortnight's Ramble To the Lakes* Jos Budworth wrote enthusiastically

101

of the beautiful daughter of the innkeeper and soon Mary Robinson was famous with visitors coming from afar to admire. Even Wordsworth and Coleridge called while on a walking tour in 1799.

In 1802 John Hatfield came to Buttermere for the char fishing. Calling himself the Honourable Alexander Augustus Hope MP he speedily courted and married Mary at Lorton Church, but within a year he was exposed as a scoundrel, an imposter and a bigamist. After his capture he was tried and hanged at Carlisle in 1803, not for these crimes but for the forgery of franking his own letters. This sensational story was all over the newspapers and a melodrama of the tale was performed in London. Wordsworth like many others was fascinated by the story and with his sister Dorothy and Coleridge visited Hatfield in prison, later referring to Mary in *The Prelude*:

> *And how the Spoiler came a 'bold bad Man'*
> *To God unfaithful, Children, Wife, and Home,*
> *And wooed the artless Daughter of the hills,*
> *And wedded her, in cruel mockery*
> *Of love and marriage bonds.*

After Hatfield's execution tourists flocked to see Mary. Southey and De Quincy both went to see her, the latter writing of her in *Recollections of the Lakes and the Lake Poets*. As they all stayed at the inn it must have been very good for trade. For Mary the story ended happily as she married a local farmer from Caldbeck, had four children and remained beautiful until her death in 1837.

High Crag from Hay Stacks

DAY 7 BUTTERMERE TO HONISTER PASS

HIGH LEVEL ROUTE	Distance 7 miles	Ascent 3,450ft
LOW LEVEL ROUTE	Distance 5¹/₂ miles	Ascent 1,450ft

ROUTE SUMMARY

High Level Route After climbing steeply from the end of Buttermere, one of the most beautiful ridges in the Lake District leads over Red Pike, High Crag and High Stile to Hay Stacks. Much of the route is rough and takes longer than expected while lingering on Hay Stacks beguiles away the time that is left.

Low Level Route A gentle stroll beside Buttermere is followed by an easy ascent up an old road to the deserted and abandoned Honister Quarries.

NOTE: The High Level Route can be joined at Scarth Gap to add on Hay Stacks, while if bad weather or blisters prevail it is only 4 miles by road from Buttermere to Honister Hause.

Facing the village of Buttermere, high above the lake, is the steep rock wall of Red Pike, High Stile and High Crag, the long ridge which divides this valley from Ennerdale. On the southern side mainly grassy slopes fall steeply to the quiet, lonely and remote valley of Ennerdale where the lower flanks are covered in the dark green of the Forestry Commission plantations. To the west the ridge declines towards the Floutern Pass over the rounded summits of Starling Dodd and Great Borne, but although their shape recalls Skiddaw Slate country, only the top of Starling Dodd is of this softer rock, and the rest is a pink granite known as granophyre. Red Pike, whose ruddy screes fall steeply to Bleaberry Tarn in its glacial combe at the foot of the crags, is also formed from the same pink rock, but High Stile, the highest of the summits, and the continuation over High Crag and Hay Stacks are made of that rock so characteristic of the Lake District, the Borrowdale Volcanics. These are the hard rocks that resisted the scouring of the glaciers to yield the jagged outlines and steep cliffs of the core of Lakeland.

Crossing the flat fields which separate Buttermere from Crummock Water, the routes divide below Red Pike where the Low Level turns to follow the shores of Buttermere. Once joined as twins, the lakes were separated by debris brought down by rivers of meltwater at the end of the Ice Age. While today a summer thunderstorm can turn the streams into boulder-trundling torrents, it is difficult to imagine the force of the water which flowed from the glaciers, glaciers which covered these summits and deposited erratics on High Stile at a height of 2,600 feet.

Buttermere and Crummock Water

From Bleaberry Tarn high above, Sourmilk Gill froths down to enter Buttermere, but so close to the outflow beck does it join that its waters have a mere brief acquaintance with the lake before hurrying on to Crummock Water. This is the first of the Lake District's three Sourmilk Gills to be met. The most celebrated of the area's waterfalls is not, however, here but round the corner where, above Crummock Water on the slopes of Starling Dodd, Scale Beck tumbles from the red granophyre at Scale Force. Falling 172 feet this is the longest waterfall in the Lake District.

After a day of brilliant sunshine on the tops, we descended to the shore of Buttermere for a swim in the cool, clear waters. This is among the purest of the Lakes. To put it in scientific terms, the pollution from phosphates in Buttermere is reckoned to be one ten-thousandth that of London's drinking water.

Climbing through the sharp-scented pines of Burtness Wood, the High Level Route emerges onto the open fellside and continues steeply to Bleaberry Tarn, where above the tarn is the junction of the red granophyre with the volcanic rocks. The path of steep scree, bright red in colour, climbs towards the ridge and emerging onto the summit of Red Pike, the hard work of the day is done.

The traverse of the ridge, though short, is a delight, from Red Pike beside the edge of Chapel Crags, over High Stile, then above Burtness Comb, long a favourite of rock climbers, and finally to High Crag. On the northern edge the cliffs and screes plunge spectacularly to Buttermere far below and across the valley are Hindscarth, Robinson and the North-Western Fells, but the

105

view that catches the attention is to the south with the giants of Lakeland, Pillar and Gable and beyond them, Sca Fell and Scafell Pike.

The ridge is a place to linger, to have lunch, to enjoy the views and then beyond High Crag, steep eroded screes slither you down to a nameless little tarn. There is a brief interlude of grass on the low summit of Seat and then after more screes Scarth Gap is reached. At certain times of the day this is one of the busiest passes in the Lake District. Nearing the end of a sunny day, just as it is going dark, a steady procession of figures may be seen wearily ascending to the pass from Ennerdale and then trudging down to Gatesgarth Farm at the head of Buttermere. These are climbers, for the crossing of Scarth Gap is a route to and from Pillar Rock and despite the ascent it is much quicker than the drive round and the long walk up Ennerdale.

Beyond Scarth Gap lies Hay Stacks. Hay Stacks is not one of the Lakeland giants, it is not even a two-thousander, but it is a fell of discoveries with a surprise around every corner. Little paths meander across its top, each one inviting detours of exploration, past silver tarns fringed with reeds and cotton grass set amid heather and rocky knolls. Here is Blackbeck Tarn, the largest, and Innominate Tarn, meaning the nameless tarn.

Hay Stacks has always been a favourite of Wainwright and it was while writing this chapter that we learned with great sadness that the man, whose books have been a constant and delightful companion, had died. In *Fellwanderer* he wrote in his inimitable style some twenty years ago:

> *And afterwards, a last long resting place by the side of Innominate Tarn on Haystacks, where the water gently laps the gravelly shore and the heather blooms and Pillar and Gable keep unfailing watch. A quiet place, a lonely place. I shall go to it for the last time, and be carried: someone who knew me in life will take me and empty me out of a little box and leave me there alone.*
> *And if you dear reader, should get a bit of grit in your boot as you are crossing Haystacks in the years to come, please treat it with respect. It might be me.*

ROUTE DESCRIPTION

JOINT ROUTE

From the Bridge Hotel in the centre of **Buttermere** go down the lane to the left of the Fish Hotel signed 'Public Bridleway Buttermere Lake'. Ahead Sourmilk Gill can be seen cascading down the hillside through the wood. Keeping to the main track and ignoring the right turn to Scale Bridge, zigzag through the fields to the lake shore and over the footbridges to enter **Burtness Wood** at a small gate where the High and Low Routes part company.

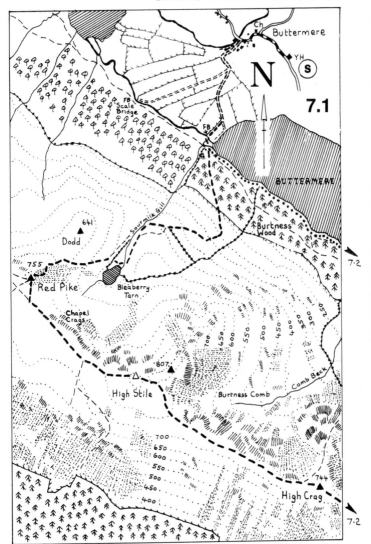

Red Pike and Bleaberry Tarn

HIGH LEVEL ROUTE

Immediately after entering the wood take the newly repaired path to Red Pike that climbs steeply through the trees. It is much easier to go up this path than to come down, it is rather like climbing a flight of stairs, and you ascend equally rapidly. In the many necessary stops for breath the view over Buttermere to the North-Western Fells expands and a gate at the top of the wood leads onto the open fellside. The path now steepens even further as it heads straight up the hillside, and the view behind extends to encompass Crummock Water. At the top of the restored section the path returns at a more gentle angle to the pink ravine of Sourmilk Gill with Red Pike at last appearing ahead. Keep to the left of the gill and the wall to reach **Bleaberry Tarn** where, as the name suggests, blueberries or bilberries can be found.

108

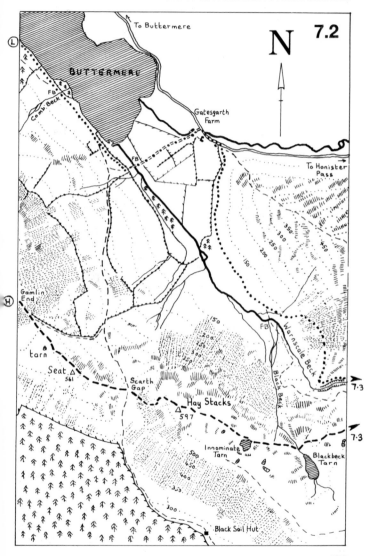

This is a convenient coffee spot where the geological differences between Red Pike and the neighbouring High Stile can clearly be seen.

The path again climbs steeply across the slopes of Dodd, which means round bare hill and zigzags up the eroded red screes to the summit of **Red Pike** which is indeed red. The rocks which formed the large cairn had been refashioned to make a windshelter on our last visit. Four of the Lake District 'waters' can be seen from here: Ennerdale Water, Loweswater, and Crummock Water, then beyond the North-Western Fells is Derwent Water. The end of Buttermere can also be seen and to the south-east the Scafells are framed between High Stile and Pillar.

A line of cairns leads south to a ruined fence which can be followed as a guide in mist, though in good weather the view is much finer by the edge. Below to the left Bleaberry Tarn lies snug in the glaciated combe beneath Chapel Crags and a brief rocky scramble brings you to a large cairn a few strides from the edge of the crags with a view of Crummock Water and Bleaberry Tarn. This cairn is popularly regarded as the summit of the fell, but the Ordnance Survey meticulously records the highest point of **High Stile** as a little further, the second cairn on the promontory a few yards from the fence corner. To the south across Ennerdale is Pillar and Pillar Rock, while further away are the Scafells.

Continuing south then east along the ridge for another mile, route-finding is easy. This is a lovely ridge walk with a feeling of being on top of the world. A gentle descent is followed by an equally gentle ascent with a line of fence posts continuing to show the route in mist, but in clear weather there are no doubts. Far below to the left is Burtness Comb, a popular haunt of rock climbers. The twin cairns of **High Crag,** each decorated with fence posts, mark the highest point and Hay Stacks now appears ahead. Surrounded by higher fells and much lower than the main ridge, with its little tarns and succession of rocky tops, it is a favourite of many fellwalkers.

The steep descent over slippery scree to the south-east is on a badly eroded path, but is made slightly easier by keeping over to the right and zigzagging down to the col where a small tarn reflects the steep face of Pillar to the south. The pink granophyre outcrops again briefly here at the Marble Stone which has a fence post embedded in the top. The intermediate grassy top of Seat provides an excuse for a brief rest before descending another, but easier and much shorter scree slope to the col at **Scarth Gap**. From the old Norse 'skarth', a gap in a ridge, this is an old pony road through the mountains. Follow the fence posts across the col to a stony path which slants right then turns left at a cairn to climb over more scree and through the crags to the summit of **Hay Stacks**. A cairn marks the highest spot at the southern end of a rocky rib on the far side of a little tarn. Great Gable and Kirk Fell attract the eye to the south-east, northwards Skiddaw is framed between the tops of Hindscarth and Robinson and to the east is the long ridge of the

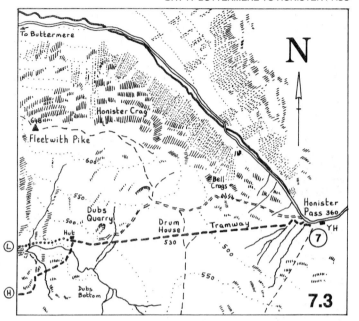

Helvellyn range.

Continuing in the same south-easterly direction the main path along the ridge follows the humps and bumps gently downhill, past Innominate Tarn to a rough section where gullies plunge steeply to Warnscale Bottom. After crossing the outflow of Blackbeck Tarn the path climbs a little and turns right before descending again to ford Warnscale Beck after half a mile. This whole area is a network of minor paths, so care must be taken in mist. Just above Warnscale Beck is **Dubbs Quarry** and the now derelict climbing hut where the Low Level Route is rejoined.

LOW LEVEL ROUTE

After entering **Burtness Wood** keep beside the shore of the lake on the permissive footpath, a broad track. At the head of the lake Fleetwith Pike is presented in dramatic profile. On the far shore is Hassness, which has an unusual feature as the lakeside path goes through a tunnel in the grounds. This was made by the owner in the nineteenth century to link the lakeside footpath and to provide work for his men in the winter. A small footpath wanders off keeping to the very edge of the lake, rejoining the main track a

111

Fleetwith Pike and Buttermere

little further on. Leaving the wood the path continues beside the lake where on the far side is the much photographed clump of Scots pines.

By forking right at the end of the lake the High Level Route may be joined at Scarth Gap, thus adding Hay Stacks to the itinerary.

Continuing to just past the head of the lake, turn left through fields and a campsite to **Gatesgarth**, which means 'Goat Pass', where the BBC television series *One Man and His Dog* was filmed in 1975.

From here Honister Hause Youth Hostel is only 2¹/₂ miles up the Honister Pass road, but the route beside Warnscale Beck to the Drum House is not much longer and is greatly to be preferred.

Walk a few yards up Honister Pass and turn right after Gatesgarth Cottage along the bridleway. The white cross above is a memorial to Fanny Mercer who was killed in 1887 while descending Fleetwith Pike. Fanny, who was a servant on holiday with her employers and was only eighteen, died from her injuries after tripping over her fell-pole, which was considered an essential item of equipment for walkers in those days. After curving round the foot of Fleetwith Pike the bridleway enters an impressive amphitheatre of crags, with even Hay Stacks looking enormous from here. Leaving the flat **Warnscale Bottom** the track makes an easy passage, ascending through rough boulders on a well-constructed old mine road. Zigzagging up the hillside beside the ravine and waterfalls of Warnscale Beck, the path becomes narrower as it climbs. This is one of the few places in the Lake District where we have found the yellow mountain saxifrage. Rounding the final bend the quarry building, once used as a climbing hut, comes into view where the High Level Route is joined at a height of 1,600 feet.

JOINT ROUTE

From the doorway of **Dubs Quarry** hut the old trackway of Moses Trod can be seen slanting across under Brandreth, while in the opposite direction Pillar towers over Hay Stacks. Dub's Quarry closed in 1932 but Keswick Mountaineering Club rebuilt the quarrymen's hut and it was opened in 1953 by George Abraham, though sadly it is becoming rapidly derelict again. Walking up the old mine road it is an easy stroll of about half a mile to the ruins of the Drum House which housed the winding gear at the head of the quarry tramway linking Dubs Quarry to the Hause. To the left are the most recent of the quarry workings and to the right across a sea of grass rises Grey Knotts. The incline which was built about 1890 points straight at Helvellyn and provides an easy descent, the eroded section at the bottom being avoided by a new path which curves left to the summit of Honister Pass and Lakeland's highest youth hostel, **Honister Hause.**

Those in search of more luxurious accommodation have an easy extra 1½ miles of downhill walking to Seatoller (see maps 8.1 and 9.1).

HONISTER PASS

The summit of Honister Pass is now strangely silent. The yard is empty, the splitting and dressing sheds closed and shuttered. A few finished slates lie abandoned by a pile of waste blocks, but now nothing moves in the yard once busy with the sound of the cutting saws. The Buttermere and Westmorland Green Slate Co Ltd is no more.

You only have to look up to Honister Crag on the slopes of Fleetwith Pike overhanging the pass, or to the screes of Yew Crag Quarry opposite on Dale Head, to see that this was a major undertaking. As the massive scars on the hillside testify, this was, until 1985, a busy working quarry.

The hillside was worked almost continuously since 1643. The slate was at first quarried from tunnels or caves and then later by opencast methods. Until 1870 the slate was brought down the hillside on wooden sledges with a man running in front to steer, a highly dangerous occupation. This method was replaced by tramways, the lines of which can be seen sloping across the rocky face, and one is now the main path down from the Drum House. At first the slate was taken to Wasdale by pony via Moses Trod and then on to Drigg near Ravenglass to be transported by sea, but in recent years lorries with their loads of slate crawled down the mountain on a modern zigzag road. The green slate was cut into blocks and split to form roofing slabs and it was also in great demand for facing buildings in London and many other cities.

The quarry workings have widened Honister Hause which was once a very narrow gap where the wind funnelled through with such great force that it has picked quarrymen from the face and hurled them to their deaths. When a hostel was built for the workers in 1927, to replace the earlier huts and barracks, it was fastened down with wire ropes. It was a rush job completed in only twenty-eight days, but the building was replaced in 1960 by the present youth hostel. The men lived in this bleak spot all week, visiting their homes only at weekends and communicating with their families during the week by carrier pigeon.

The old road over the pass which served the quarries was open to the public as a toll road and was surfaced for the first time in 1934. After the Second World War, when the road was to be modernised and adopted by the council, the owner refused to sell for less than £2,000. This was considered far too much and so the present road was built. The old toll road fell into disuse and it now makes a pleasant route for walkers. Ward Lock's *Red Guide* describes the new road over Honister Pass:

> *The scene of so many struggles between car and contour in the past, but now equipped with a well-made modern road which reduces the toil and danger to a minimum though the gradients are still severe.*

At the foot of Honister Pass the hamlet of Seatoller is only a handful of farms and miners' cottages. There is no pub but the Yew Tree is a licensed restaurant. There is a large car park and a regular bus service to Keswick and in the information centre at Seatoller Barn, talks and slide shows are given in the summer.

The head of Newlands Beck

HIGH LEVEL ROUTE	Distance 10 miles	Ascent 2,100ft
LOW LEVEL ROUTE	Distance 6½ miles	Ascent 350ft

ROUTE SUMMARY

High Level Route With a gradual easy ascent the summit of Dale Head is soon reached. The route then drops steeply to Dalehead Tarn before following the mainly grassy ridge of High Spy and Maiden Moor high above Borrowdale all the way to Cat Bells. Descending to the village of Grange the Low Route is joined to walk beside the River Derwent to Rosthwaite.

Low Level Route This takes the old road down Borrowdale past Castle Crag to Grange and then follows the River Derwent back to Rosthwaite.

NOTE: If last night was spent at Seatoller this will add 1½ miles and 800 feet of ascent to the High Level Route, but it takes under an hour to return to the top of the pass. The Low Level Route will, however, be shortened by 1 mile, in fact, by cheating and walking straight there you could arrive at Rosthwaite for coffee time.

To the west of Derwent Water rises the cone of Cat Bells, the objective of many a family outing from Keswick and the northernmost top of the ridge which divides the vale of Newlands from Borrowdale. Further south the ridge rises to Maiden Moor and High Spy, whose grassy tops contrast with rocky sides which fall steeply to the valleys, while looking down on the head of Newlands is Dale Head the highest summit of the day. After the gradual ascent of Dale Head, the descent to Dalehead Tarn is steep, but the continuation along the ridge is both easy and delightful. To the left precipitous drops fall to Newlands over Miners Crag, Red Crag and Eel Crag on the flanks of High Spy. To the right far below is Derwent Water, its surface rippled with lines drawn by the sailing boats and the launches which circle the lake, calling at the long wooden piers which stretch into the deeper water.

Borrowdale, or as it was called in Viking times, Borgar dalr, the valley of the fort, is one of the great treasures of the Lake District. A steep-sided wooded valley of oak, ash, birch and hazel with hawthorn, blackthorn, rowan, elder and holly, its autumn colours set it off to natural perfection. But it isn't natural. Like so much of Lakeland it is the product of man and almost by chance has become what we see today. Few of the woods are the original oakwoods. Felling started in prehistoric times and was completed by the early Norse farming communities and, if left to the sheep, the hillsides would still be bare as no tree seedling can survive for long in an area grazed by

Abbot's Bay, Derwent Water

these mowing machines. Much of the present woodland was planted in the seventeenth century, then fenced and managed as coppiced woodland to provide fuel for the smelting furnaces. The fuel was charcoal and small level clearings can still be found in the woods where the charcoal burners built their mounds of slowly smouldering timber.

Borrowdale starts at the hamlet of Grange where a fine two-arched stone bridge crosses the River Derwent. Much of Borrowdale was bought by Furness Abbey in 1209, the estate extending right up into the hills and including Great Gable. To the west was still deer forest and to the east the land was owned by Fountains Abbey. The name Grange refers to its function as a monastic grange, a grain store, and this was the chief settlement in the valley. Although the name was first recorded in 1396 it seems likely that this crossing point on the River Derwent would have been settled much earlier.

Above Grange the valley suddenly narrows and squeezes its way between the cliffs of High Spy to the west and Grange Fell to the east. These narrows are known as the Jaws of Borrowdale and in the eighteenth century very few travellers penetrated beyond this point into the savage wilderness beyond. *This valley, so replete with hideous grandeur* wrote William Gilpin in 1772. Defending this gateway is Castle Crag, an isolated rock tower rising from the surrounding woods. The summit of Castle Crag was the site of an earthwork fort, built to defend the British against the Romans. It must have been a good position and since then much of the face has been quarried,

117

making it even steeper and grander. Castle Crag would have all been quarried away were it not for the intervention of Lord William Gordon who bought it at the end of the eighteenth century to save it from destruction.

On the eastern slopes of Castle Crag is a quarry with several caves. The uppermost two are joined by a short tunnel and here Millican Dalton, an eccentric, made his summer home. The higher cave was his bedroom and the lower and larger cave his living room and entertaining room. He acted as a guide to the fells and was a well-known character in the district during the 1930s. Inscribed on the rock face outside the upper cave entrance is the motto, DON'T WASTE WORRDS. JUMP TO CONCLUSIONS. The spelling was a little joke with a friend from Glasgow who did the carving.

On the opposite side of the River Derwent is the Bowder Stone which has been a tourist attraction for over two hundred years. This is a 36-foot high 2,000-ton boulder which is balanced on one corner. It was 'improved' for the tourists by digging a hole underneath so they could shake hands under 'the largest fragment of rock in the world' with a specially employed little old woman. A wooden staircase of twenty-nine steps has been built so people may climb to the top. The old road beside the stone was made in 1842 and was the first up the valley. In 1910, along with Grange Fell the Bowder Stone was purchased by the National Trust.

Rosthwaite, so often a hurried point of call to buy stamps or postcards, a newspaper or food on one of our backpacking trips, is also a place of renewed meetings. Some fifteen years ago while passing the post office in the car we glimpsed an acquaintance of Anne's who had moved away. We joined them for a walk and our friendship has grown with the years. In those days their three girls and our two boys made the numbers up to nine, but the girls always seemed to be the keenest to get to the fell tops. It was a long time before we learnt their secret. After a day of heavy, sultry heat we were about to descend into the valley, but one last summit tempted. "Who's coming?" we asked. "I'll come for the money," replied one of the girls. There was a sudden silence. The secret was out, - 10p per thousand feet! Our boys looked enquiringly at Anne. "That's only for girls," she announced firmly. All this was several years ago and last year we climbed Scafell Pike together. This time a boyfriend, a girlfriend and a husband joined the party, but as far as we know not a single bribe was offered or received.

The climb up the long grassy slopes from Honister Pass to the summit of Dale Head skirts Yewcrag quarries which, like the ones on the western side of the pass, produced an attractive green slate. Dale Head looks down on the Newlands valley and the sides of the mountain and those of High Spy and Maiden Moor are penetrated everywhere by old mine workings. The Dale Head mines were first worked by the Germans in the sixteenth century. The copper was taken down to the lake at Hawse End, where the loading bay is marked on maps as Copperheap Hill, and then by boat across the lake to a smelter built at Brigham near Keswick.

Copper and lead were the chief minerals of the Borrowdale mines and of these the Goldscope Mine in Newlands valley beneath Maiden Moor was the biggest. Worked for copper from early in the thirteenth century, Goldscope was at its zenith in the sixteenth century when German miners were brought in for their expertise. The Germans, probably for their own security, lived on Derwent Isle, safely surrounded by water, but as suspicion of the foreigners abated they married into local families. The copper was marked with the King's mark at the Receiving House which was built, or rather rebuilt, from an earlier building in Keswick in 1571. It is now the Moot Hall. The smelter at Brigham was destroyed by Cromwell's troops during the Civil War and the mine was then closed. After a brief period of renewed activity in the late seventeenth century Goldscope again lay dormant, but in the mid-nineteenth century lead was discovered and for a few years the mine was once more prosperous. The First World War again saw production, but mining ceased in 1920 and now little sign remains of this once major industry in the fields below Low Snab Farm.

The largest of the lead mines in Borrowdale was at Brandlehow on the shores of Derwent Water. As the lead miners followed the line of ore down to the lakeside they had to contend with one of the miners' biggest problems, water. Water-wheels were built to drive the pumps, but until the coming of steam power in the nineteenth century it was a losing battle. In the late nineteenth century, while steam drove the pumps, a huge thirty-foot diameter water-wheel was built beside the lake to power the crushing mill. Even this was dwarfed by the great wheel at Uzzicar near the village of Stair in the Newlands valley.

At the end of a long day on the Borrowdale fells we came down to the shore of Derwent Water to board the launch back across the lake to our waiting car. As we took our seats among the other fellwalkers and family groups, a small boy turned to his mother. It had obviously been a boring day, but now there was a note of real interest in his voice. "Look Mam!", he cried. "A dead duck!" As all eyes turned to the water and the two pathetic upturned webbed feet, his mother's voice rose above the conversation; "We've brought you all t'way to t'Lake District and all you can say is, 'Look Mam, there's a dead duck!'"

ROUTE DESCRIPTION

HIGH LEVEL ROUTE

From **Honister Hause** Youth Hostel cross the road and climb straight up the fellside opposite on the obvious path beside the fence. Looking down the pass there is a grandstand view of the face of Fleetwith Pike with its tramways and tunnels and far down the valley a glimpse of Buttermere and Crummock

119

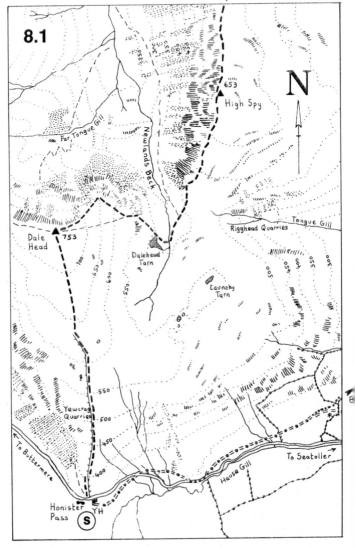

Water. Yewcrag Quarries too, on this side of the road, extend far up the mountain with open chasms, disused inclines, ruined buildings and vast piles of slate waste generated by the miners. For every ton of usable slate up to ten tons of spoil were created and dumped on the fellsides, but time has mellowed the waste tips which are now colonised by plants including the alpine lady's mantle. The new fence ceases above the highest workings and the path continues along the line of old fence posts to the last one which stands solitary on the summit of **Dale Head**. The stone column may be there or not, there is a constant battle between cairn builders and cairn wreckers. On our last visit, a brilliantly sunny March day, the column stood six feet high and from it there are long views down into the valley of Newlands Beck with its disused mines and beyond is the Skiddaw range. To the south lie the Scafells and Gable, further west is Kirk Fell and then the huge bulk of Pillar, while to the east is the long ridge of Fairfield, Helvellyn and the Dodds.

From Dale Head follow the edge down eastwards and then after veering away to the right the path becomes indistinct as it descends to the boggy surrounds of **Dalehead Tarn**. Passing to the left of the tarn by a sheepfold the path goes between two knolls to cross Newlands Beck which flows through a rocky gorge. It is then an easy uphill walk of just over half a mile to the summit of High Spy. On the opposite side of the Newlands valley a zigzag mine path rises to the left of Far Tongue Gill above the old copper workings of Dalehead Mine. Further down the valley is Castlenook Mine, a small lead mine which was worked from 1860 until 1918. **High Spy** has a fine cairn and good distant views of the long Helvellyn range to the east and to the north-west lie Grasmoor, Eel Crags and Grisedale Pike. Just past the summit a tempting little path leads out onto a fine rocky rib with an airy view of the Newlands valley far below.

Most of the hard work of the day has now been done and it is an easy stroll of about half a mile along the path which follows the left side of the ridge to High Spy North Top. This is a rocky knoll, topped with a cairn from which there are fine views of Derwent Water. The path continues as a broad sweep over **Maiden Moor**, descending so gently on easy grassy slopes that walking seems effortless. The top of this undistinguished spot is by-passed by an alternative path. It isn't really a summit as it has so little ascent, but the highest point is by the edge and is marked with a few stones. To the west on the other side of Newlands Beck can clearly be seen the old spoil heaps of the Goldscope Mine at Scope End. This was a very old lead and copper mine. It was called Gottesgab, God's Gift, by the German miners who were brought over in 1564. For there to be such a vast quantity of waste from such a small opening, the end of the ridge must surely be hollow and in fact there is over a mile of tunnels within the hill.

The ridge continues, descending at a somewhat steeper angle to the col at **Hause Gate**. Below to the right on the shore of Brandlehow Bay was the

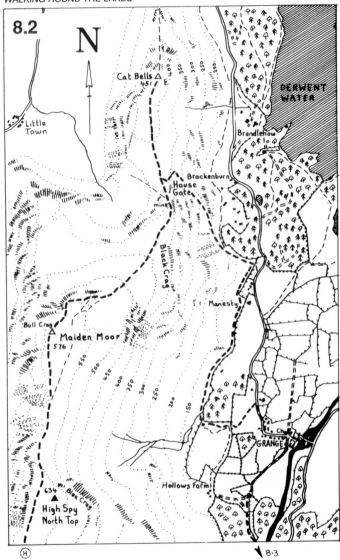

8.2

N

Cat Bells △
451

Little
Town

DERWENT
WATER

Brandlehow

Brackenburn
Hause
Gate
mine

Black Crag

Manesty

Bull Crag

△ Maiden Moor
576

550
500
450
400
350
300
250
200
150

Ch.
GRANGE

Hollows Farm

634 Blea Crag
▲
High Spy
North Top

Ⓗ

↘ 8·3

122

High Spy from Dale Head

Brandlehow Lead Mine which although very profitable, was plagued by flooding and the mine was abandoned in 1891. To the left is Yewthwaite Lead Mine, which by Lake District standards is fairly young. Dating from the mid-nineteenth century, it was worked for nearly fifty years.

A final sharp pull up leads to the summit of **Cat Bells**. Although at 1,600 feet this is not one of Lakeland's giants, rising straight from the shore of Derwent Water it looks a challenging objective. For many visitors to Keswick this must be their first Lake District fell and it is so often visited that the summit is quite bare and balding, like a much loved teddy bear. We had the polished rocks to ourselves in March, our only companion a small bird energetically taking a dust bath. From here you look down on Derwent Water and its islands, but soon the eye is drawn to the higher fells. Skiddaw and Blencathra rise aloof above Keswick, seeming near but so huge that no figures can be discerned on their tops.

Returning to Hause Gate a good path zigzags downhill towards the end of the lake. Below is Brackenburn where Hugh Walpole, the New Zealand-born author of *The Herries Chronicle*, lived for part of each year from 1923 until his death in 1941. It was originally a bungalow, but when growing trees blocked his view an extra storey was added.

Just before joining the road turn right at a gate and follow above the fence to pass the wood behind Manesty Cottages. The path runs along the hillside with Castle Crag ahead standing sentinel at the Jaws of Borrowdale. After passing a narrow ravine cross the stream to a stile and follow the wall down to a gate. Slanting back across the next field to the Borrowdale Gates Hotel, turn right along the road into **Grange**. The house on the right called Copperfield has no connection with mining but was built by Hugh Walpole with money received from a film about the book by Dickens.

LOW LEVEL ROUTE

From **Honister Hause** follow the old toll road east, first to the right and then to the left of the new Honister Pass road. The old road then briefly joins the new before passing high above Seatoller with the view down Borrowdale opening out ahead. Just before a small plantation of larch trees, take the bridleway at a low-set sign, going left to a little gate. Following the path above the wall Castle Crag appears ahead and to the right in the valley below is the village of Rosthwaite. After the third footbridge, the path climbs to join a broad track and at the top of the rise Derwent Water and Skiddaw come into view.

Ahead to the right are the steep fortress-like rocks of **Castle Crag**, but although it can be omitted the top is reached in only a few minutes and is well worth the effort. Turn off to the right where the wall abuts a crag and follow the small path round beside a fence to a wall where a ladder stile leads to piles of discarded slate. A path zigzags up through the slate tips to the old quarry and ruined buildings nearly at the top of the crag and then continues easily to the summit. This is a surprise, a broad lawn-like expanse surrounded by sheer cliffs.

Castle Crag was given to the National Trust by Sir William Hamer as a war memorial to the men of Borrowdale and to his son John who was killed in action in the First World War, aged twenty-one. From this high vantage point Derwent Water is seen stretching away down to Keswick with Skiddaw rising imperiously beyond. Close at hand the long ridge of High Spy and Maiden Moor dwarfs this tiny summit and to the south are the giants of central Lakeland, Great Gable, Sca Fell and Scafell Pike.

To descend, retrace your steps through the spoil heaps, but instead of crossing the ladder stile continue down to a step stile. A small ladder aids the drop over a wall and the path continues down to the old road past a commemorative seat to Agnes, the wife of Sir William Hamer, who died in 1939 leaving the land surrounding Castle Crag to the National Trust in memory of her husband.

Continue for another half mile on the old road, which has been recently repaired, to enter the wood at a gate and descend to the **River Derwent**. The village of Grange is half a mile downstream, but the visit can be omitted as you return the same way.

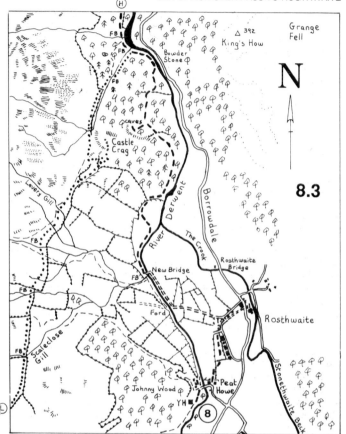

GRANGE

The little hamlet of Grange, its cottages clustered round the village green and described as "one of the prettiest villages in the Lake District", makes a pleasant interlude in the day's walk. Endowed with two tea shops and a hotel, the amenities are completed by the public toilets and a telephone box, but the post office, shop and village school are now gone. The fine stone bridge, which was built in 1675, spans the River Derwent connecting the village to the road up Borrowdale. Here is the bus stop and the Lakeland Rural Industries, a pleasant gift shop and gallery. Grange church was built in 1860 by Miss Heathcote, a local benefactor, and beside the bridge is the Methodist chapel which was built in 1894.

JOINT ROUTE

From the village of **Grange**, take the track opposite the church which leads up Borrowdale, turning left to enter the wood and passing through a campsite which is usually full of tents. Reaching the river the path crosses a couple of footbridges to join the **Low Level Route** at a signposted path junction. From here head upstream on the path signed 'Rosthwaite' which soon curves away from the River Derwent. Grange Fell on the far side of the river was bought by the National Trust in 1910 and King's How was named by Princess Louise in memory of her brother, King Edward VII. If the trees have shed their leaves it is possible to make out the huge bulk of the Bowder Stone, an erratic left by the retreating glaciers. At the highest point on the path fork right to visit **Millican Dalton's Cave** in the quarry below Castle Crag. Passing a large cave which has a huge boulder cleft by an ash tree at the entrance, climb a little higher to the twin caves in which Millican spent the summer months in the years before the last war.

Return to the junction and continue descending gently through the wood then go through the fields to a broad path by the reinforced river bank and on to New Bridge. A concessionary path on the west bank leads directly to the youth hostel in half a mile, but for **Rosthwaite** cross the bridge and follow the wide track past the stepping stones to enter the village by Yew Tree Farm.

The shop and main road are to the left, but for the youth hostel turn right to follow the lane past the cottages to a footpath which passes behind the new houses on the right signed 'Longthwaite Youth Hostel'. The footpath follows the edge of the field to a stile and then cuts across the corner of the next field, where huge boulders have been incorporated into the walls. A field gate leads onto the lane at a stile by Peat Howe. Turn right to cross the river to Longthwaite Farm and up the track to **Longthwaite Youth Hostel.**

ROSTHWAITE

Standing on The How, a rocky intrusion into the flat valley floor of the River Derwent, is the village of Rosthwaite. The brilliant white statesmen-farms shaded by yew trees are, like the valley walls, made from smooth boulders gathered from the fields when first they were cleared and even the council houses have been built of local stone. Nokka House, which is now the post office and general stores, was once an inn and the old Salving House opposite belongs to the Fell and Rock Climbing Club. The village institute which was built in 1922 keeps busy with local events. Tourism and farming are the main industries of Borrowdale and the largest landowner is the National Trust.

Longthwaite Youth Hostel, purpose-built in 1939, is a timber framed construction of Canadian red cedar and was enlarged in 1965. The nearby Longthwaite Bridge was built in 1899 to replace an earlier one which had been swept away by floods. Behind the hostel is Johnny Wood, a very old coppiced oak wood, parts of which have existed for centuries and may, in fact, never have been felled. On its rocky floor are found mosses, liverworts and ferns which have probably grown here since the last Ice Age. The wood, although mainly of oak has sycamore and a few other trees and shrubs, and is a Site of Special Scientific Interest belonging to the National Trust.

Hazel Bank just across the river at the northern end of the village is supposedly the fictional home of Walpole's Rogue Herries. In the first chapter of *Rogue Herries* the first novel of the series, Francis arrives in Rosthwaite with his small son, David:

> They moved on upwards over a little hill with hills on their left side and the flooded gleaming river on their right. It was all very quiet and still. The storm had altogether died away. No one spoke, and the only sound was the hoofs of the horses, now soft, now sharp. The scene was now to David, who had only all his life seen flat and shallow country, incredibly wonderful.
>
> They were passing through a gateway of high rock into a little valley, still as a man's hand and bleached under the moon, but guarded by a ring of mountains that seemed to David gigantic. The moonlight made them larger and marked the shadows and lines of rock like bands of jagged iron. In colour they were black against the soft lighted sky and the myriads of silver stars. A little wind, not sharp and cold as it had been before, but gentle and mild, whispered across the valley.

Peat Howe, Rosthwaite

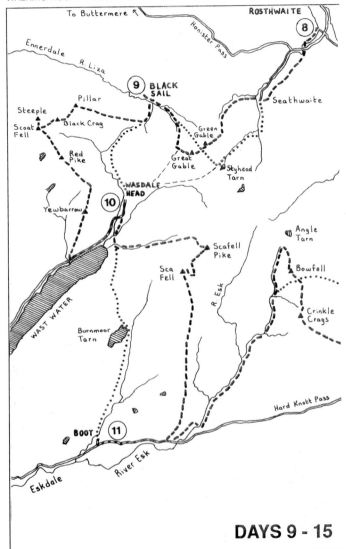

DAYS 9 - 15

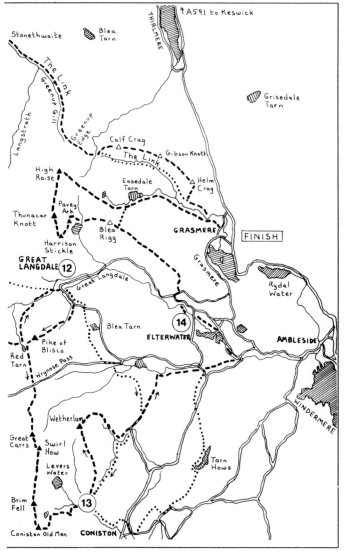

Great Gable from Scafell Pike

DAY 9 ROSTHWAITE TO BLACK SAIL (OR WASDALE HEAD)

HIGH LEVEL ROUTE	Black Sail	Distance 6 miles	Ascent 2,750ft
	(Wasdale	Distance 7 miles	Ascent 2,750ft)
LOW LEVEL ROUTE	Black Sail	Distance 6 miles	Ascent 2,050ft
	(Wasdale	Distance 6½ miles	Ascent 1,150ft)

NOTE: Although it is the Lake District's simplest youth hostel, Black Sail Hut is very popular and as there is no other accommodation at the head of Ennerdale, an alternative finish is described which brings you to Wasdale Head.

ROUTE SUMMARY

Both routes lead at first to the hamlet of Seathwaite where they divide.

High Level Route The ascent beside Sourmilk Gill, especially attractive after rain, leads up into the hanging valley of Gillercomb. Green Gable precedes the rough scramble up and down the much rockier Great Gable and then, after descending to Beck Head, the route turns down either to Ennerdale or Wasdale. It is quite a short day, but takes longer than expected as much of the way is rough underfoot.

Low Level Route Taking the Styhead Pass the route crosses Stockley Bridge and then climbs to Styhead Tarn. With Ennerdale as the destination the route lies over Windy Gap, while for Wasdale, Lingmell Beck leads down to the valley.

The distinctive shape of Great Gable is easily identified on the skyline of countless distant views of the hills, but while many mountain names are derived from Norse terminology bestowed by early settlers, Gable has no such grand pretentions and is so named simply because it looks like the gable end of a house. Some house! Nearly three thousand feet from its foundations to the rocky ridge of its roof, Great Gable not only attracts the eye, but from every side, from Wasdale, from Ennerdale, from Honister and from Seathwaite, its disciples come. The ascent from Seathwaite is one of the best. Everyone has heard of this, the wettest inhabited place in England and with an average annual rainfall of around 130 inches it certainly is on the damp side compared with the hamlet of Grange half-way down Borrowdale which boasts ninety inches, while poor Keswick can only produce a paltry fifty-eight. But fortunately there are not many more rainy days at Seathwaite than elsewhere, it just rains harder in a more determined sort of way when it does. In such conditions the approach beside Sourmilk Gill will be enjoyed

131

to the full, a raging white foam of water. This is only one of Lakeland's three Sourmilk Gills, the others being in Buttermere and Easedale. Such repetition is commonplace and although there is only one Great Gable, the Lake District possesses six Mosedales and no less than twenty-six Raven Crags.

Despite its inhospitable terrain the summit of Great Gable, rough rock and boulders, lichens and moss, is a place of pilgrimage where walkers, climbers and tourists congregate around the small and insignificant cairn. This is it, the goal of the expedition and while the approach is everything and the final attainment nothing, everyone postpones leaving the top, for to go down is to make an end of it. So lunch is eaten, the view is admired and when it can no longer be delayed, all descend reluctantly to the distant valleys.

Every year, on Remembrance Sunday, two minutes' silence is observed on the summit by crowds of walkers and climbers who come whatever the weather to stand beside the cairn. Poppies are laid at the base of the plaque, a relief map of the 3,000 acres which were given to the National Trust by members of the Fell and Rock Climbing Club:

> *In glorious & happy memory of those whose names are inscribed below members of this club who died for their country in the European War 1914-1918. These fells were acquired by their fellow-members & by them vested in the National Trust for the use & enjoyment of the people of our land for all time.*

In 1989 the National Trust won a medal of honour from Europa Nostra (a federation formed to protect Europe's cultural and natural heritage) for the work done on the path to Sty Head. The track, which was maintained as a packhorse route until as late as 1930 but had become a river of scree, has been restored by over 1,000 days of voluntary labour taking a year to complete. Following this old way, first mentioned in records in the thirteenth century and surfaced and raised above the surrounding land in the seventeenth century, Styhead Tarn comes into view beneath the cliffs of Great End. To the right rise the rough slopes of Great Gable, while to the left is Seathwaite Fell on whose summit is Sprinkling Tarn, one of the loveliest tarns in the Lakes. That a road should be driven through all this beauty is unthinkable, yet as recently as 1919 'progress' demanded that one was needed to avoid the 45-mile drive round to Wasdale and the cost was to be only £50,000. Fortunately there were many who objected to the scheme and it was turned down.

Seathwaite, a hamlet of no more than a couple of cottages with farm buildings, has a telephone, toilet, campsite and tearoom. A notice beside the barn on a recent visit announced "Dogs chasing sheep will be shot. Dogs shot to date 12". In 1966 an unusually severe storm caused the banks of the beck to break and floodwater, which also damaged Stockley Bridge, streamed through the farmyard and buildings. The repair work by the National Trust was not completed until 1986.

Stockley Bridge

As we paused beside Sourmilk Gill, where the rocks are smoothed both by the glacial action of over ten thousand years ago and more recently by the passage of several tens of thousands of feet, we looked down on Seathwaite. There seemed to be more than the usual number of vehicles jammed side by side along the verge and surely at least one of them was a police car? From across the valley came the sound of hounds. It was the hunt, but it was also the hunt saboteurs. A rather feeble tantara came from a huntsman's horn, but it was no huntsman who sat forlornly on the rocks above, just a rather weary hunt saboteur who had given up the chase. In the distance and moving strongly and surely across the fellside, the red-coated huntsman and his pack had already left the followers over a mile behind.

On the northern slopes of Great Gable is the path of Moses Trod. Moses was a legendary whisky distiller and on a ledge high on Gable Crag is a roofless smuggler's hut. Discovered in the 1890s, it was thought to be where Moses had his illicit whisky still, but this romantic legend is unlikely to be true as there is no running water nearby. It was possibly built to hide stolen wad, the graphite which was mined in Borrowdale.

Mining for wad started in Borrowdale in 1555, and it was probably then worked continuously until its closure at the end of the nineteenth century. Black lead, plumbago, or wad as it was known by the miners, had many outlets in industry as well as being used for black leading stoves and its discovery led to the founding of the pencil factory at Braithwaite in 1790. In the eighteenth century it was so valuable that an armed guard was mounted at the mine to prevent theft. The wad was sorted and washed in sheds at Seathwaite Farm where there was also accommodation for the miners. Old levels and an open shaft are strung out in a line up the fellside opposite the farm and pieces of wad can be found on the spoil heaps.

Standing apart from the surrounding fells, Great Gable is steep on all sides, but none more so than the Wasdale face which plunges in a steep scree slope of nearly two-and-a-half thousand feet to the intake walls of Wasdale Head. There is one break in the slope, rocks so high on the face that they seem insignificant and inconsequential from below, but closer at hand these sheer rock walls appear their true size. It was here that rock climbing in England began when Walter Haskett-Smith, climbing solo, first ascended the massive isolated stone pinnacle of Napes Needle. Fifty years later in 1936, to celebrate the anniversary of that first ascent and aged seventy-four, he repeated the feat to the applause of around 300 onlookers. As he reached the top, one of them shouted "Tell us a story." His confident reply floated down on the mountain air: "There is no other story, this is the top storey."

ROUTE DESCRIPTION

JOINT ROUTE

From Longthwaite Youth Hostel at **Rosthwaite** follow the River Derwent upstream towards Seatoller, then after crossing some slanting rocky slabs beside the river, the path enters the wood. On the opposite bank is a little cliff where the river has cut into the glacial moraine exposing the boulders, clays and gravels. In the field beyond turn left to cross Folly Bridge which has an unusual asymmetrical arch. On a slab tucked out of sight beside the bridge is the inscription:

> *This bridge was built at the expense of John Braithwaite of Seatoller in the year of our Lord 1781 by Thomas Hayton and Richard Bownels*
>
> *Account this Folly You have done*
> *As you have neither Wife nor Son*
> *Daughter I have, God give her grace*
> *And Heaven for her Resting Place*

It cost him twenty-five pounds.

On reaching **Mountain View**, a row of eight houses which was built for quarry workers late in the nineteenth century, go straight across the road and down the lane opposite towards Thornythwaite Farm which sits elevated on a morainic ridge out of reach of the floods. Further on, the flanking right wall is immensely broad as this was a useful way of disposing of surplus stones when the land was cleared.

When the road bends sharp right through a hidden gate to the farm, take the footpath which follows beside the wall all the way to **Seathwaite**. To the left the slopes of Thornythwaite Fell tumble huge boulders into the fields and on the flanks of Seatoller Fell, on the far side of the valley, can be seen the spoil heaps of the graphite mine.

HIGH LEVEL ROUTE

At Seathwaite turn right in front of the cottages and then left through the archway opposite signed 'Footpath' where a stone-walled track leads across to a footbridge. Climbing to the left of **Sourmilk Gill** on a newly repaired path, this steep scrambling approach is a popular route to Great Gable with the white foam of the beck tumbling down from the valley above. The path zigzags up with a brief scramble over glacier-smoothed rocks to a gate, then continues above the gill into Gillercomb which, although a glacial valley, is bereft of a tarn. It is then a gentle ascent until the final section up eroded pink scree to the ridge where a detour left to the summit of Base Brown, an out-and-back on a grassy path, is an optional extra for peak baggers.

It is now a steep climb of 600 feet on a good path to Green Gable summit and near the top the path is joined by another from Honister Pass. Just below the cairn is a wind shelter, but few take much notice of the stony summit of

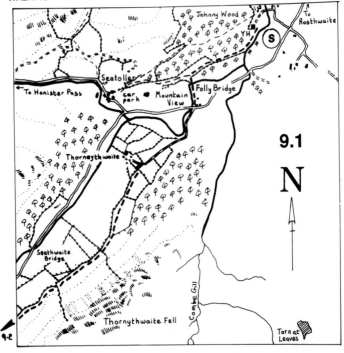

Green Gable which is dominated by its big brother Great Gable on whose shaded northern face is Gable Crag. To the north-west Ennerdale stretches into the distance and rising above the conifers is Pillar and the mass of Pillar Rock. Many of the high fells are now in view including all the 3,000-foot tops, with Skiddaw away to the north, the long Helvellyn ridge forming the skyline to the east and to the south the rugged shape of the Scafells.

Rather slippery and eroded red screes lead down to the cairn at **Windy Gap** to cross the Low Level Route. Although it is another 500 feet of steep ascent to Great Gable summit, it is an interesting scramble over rocks and boulders which maintains interest until the angle eases and a line of cairns leads over the bouldery top to the highest point. Set in the summit rocks of **Great Gable** is a bronze plaque, a memorial to the twenty members of the Fell and Rock Climbing Club who were killed in the war.

Perched on the rocks above is a small cairn where one day in March, for the first time ever on this summit, we ate our lunch in complete solitude, our

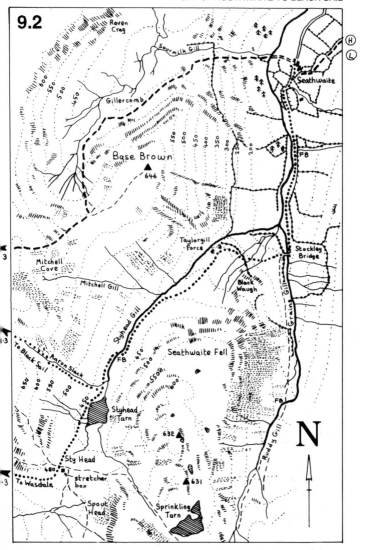

9.2

only company a scattering of orange peel. Usually the top is crowded with walkers, climbers, picknickers and tourists for it exerts a magnetic appeal to all who walk these fells. Great Gable, nearly 350 feet higher than its little brother, is not only easily recognisable from afar, but is itself an excellent vantage point. To the north, east and south the view takes in almost the whole of Lakeland, while to the west the fells surrounding Wast Water and hitherto masked by Gable itself can now be seen. To the south-west, 150 yards down from the summit and overlooking Wast Water, is the Westmorland Cairn which was built in 1876 by two brothers, the father and uncle of the late Colonel 'Rusty' Westmorland, to mark what they considered to be the finest view in the whole of the Lake District.

Descents from Gable can be a little tricky in mist, so be sure to locate the line of cairns heading north-west which indicates a safe way down. The path descends over huge rough boulders, avoiding the scree to the left and the even steeper slopes to the right, until **Beck Head** is reached with its seasonal tarns. The route now divides with the option of staying either in Wasdale or at the tiny youth hostel of Black Sail.

For **Black Sail Hut** descend rightwards from Beck Head to join the path down the grassy tongue between two gills into the head of Ennerdale. Crossing the infant River Liza where the streams meet, the Low Level Route is joined and the path on the northern bank is then followed down to the youth hostel.

With **Wasdale Head** as the destination turn left just before the Beck Head col is reached and then follow a small, very stony path across the screes high above Gable Beck. The path then descends the grassy rib of Gavel Neese to a gate in the wall and down to a footbridge where a track leads through the fields to Wasdale.

LOW LEVEL ROUTE

On reaching **Seathwaite** turn left on the bridleway to **Styhead Pass.** This gated broad track, once an important causeway, metalled and raised above the surrounding land, heads up the valley past the larch plantations and the grassy mounds of debris left when the glaciers retreated some 10,000 years ago. To the left are the lower slopes of Glaramara and on the right the massive fell is Base Brown which, although it is little more than a spur of Green Gable, looks very impressive from here. The valley now divides with the left branch climbing to Esk Hause, while to the right, the white streak of Taylorgill Force marks the route to Sty Head. Crossing **Stockley Bridge**, an attractive little packhorse bridge, the newly repaired path zigzags up the front of Seathwaite Fell and through a restored wall to pass a small plantation above Taylorgill Force. Continue beside Styhead Gill to Airy's Bridge then cross it and follow the stream up to **Styhead Tarn**, a popular high-level campsite with usually at least one small tent pitched beside its waters.

9.3

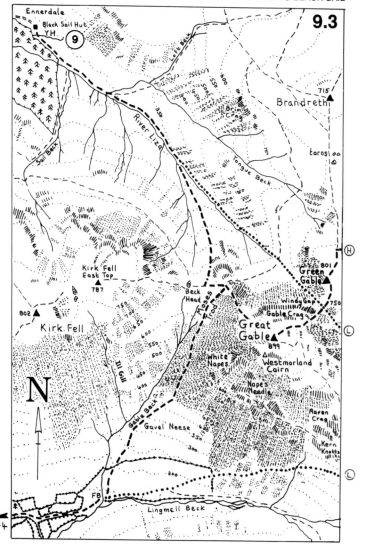

Ennerdale

Black Sail Hut
YH.

⑨

Late Beck

Brin
Crag

Brandreth

715

River Liza

Sail Beck

Tongue Beck

Tarns

Green
Gable

801

Kirk Fell
East Top

787

Beck
Head

Windy Gap

750

Gable Crag

802

Kirk Fell

750

700

650

600

550

500

Gable
Great

899

N

White
Napes

Westmorland
Cairn

Napes
Needle

Raven
Crag

Gavel Neese

Gable Beck

350

300

Kern
Knotts

200

FB

Lingmell Beck

0·4

Styhead Tarn and Great End

For **Wasdale Head** the route passes Styhead Tarn and climbs past the stretcher box to a crossroads where the path to the left climbs to Sprinkling Tarn, the one to the right to Gable and a big cairn marks the path to Wasdale. This was once an important crossing of the ways where there was a shelter for the drivers of the packhorse trains. Keep straight on and just round the corner is a breathtaking view down Wasdale. To the left is Great End, the Corridor Route slanting across its slopes, and Lingmell with the deep ravine of Piers Gill. The path descends to the right of Lingmell Beck and after crossing a stream Napes Needle may be glimpsed to the right and then a little further, the Cat Rock. The path then takes you down to the valley and Wasdale Head.

However, for **Black Sail Hut** there is still more climbing to reach Windy Gap between Green Gable and Great Gable, so from the outflow of Styhead Tarn, turn right up toward the dip in the skyline. At first there is no sign of a path, but one soon appears beside the stream coming down from the screes of Aaron Slack. Slack means screes and it is a steep climb to reach Windy Gap, but if the day has turned out fine after all the High Level Route, which crosses here, can be joined to climb Great Gable.

On reaching **Windy Gap** a backward glance reveals Styhead Tarn far below and Sprinkling Tarn and other little silver tarns on Seathwaite Fell.

Beyond Seathwaite Fell is Allen Crags with Great End to the right, its face scored by the deep cleft of Skew Gill, while to the south-east the Langdale Pikes are seen from the rear. As you start to descend from the red col towards Ennerdale the long ridge ahead is High Stile, High Crag and Hay Stacks and to the left Pillar Rock is silhouetted on the skyline.

A path down slithery red scree descends into Stone Cove, but when it does a disappearing trick the stream ahead points the way to Black Sail Hut. Crossing the narrow path of Moses Trod the infant River Liza, whose name means 'bright water', is joined and soon there is a little path to follow beside the stream, whose sparkling clear water cascades down over cushions of moss towards the tiny speck of Black Sail Hut in the valley below. As the grass-covered moraines are reached, the High Level Route from Beck Head is joined for the last mile of riverside walking to the **Black Sail Youth Hostel.**

ENNERDALE

The long narrow valley of Ennerdale, nearly eight miles from its remote head beneath the slopes of Kirk Fell and Great Gable, to the foot of Ennerdale Water occupying an ice-gouged hollow at the bottom of the dale, is almost deserted. As the climate improved towards the end of the Ice Age, meltwater dammed up by the ice which covered the Irish Sea formed a huge lake in Ennerdale, reaching up the valley almost as far as the upper limit of the present forestry plantations. Gradually the glacier melted depositing moraines at the head of the valley which are now grass-covered mounds, and the level of the lake fell in stages leaving terraces on the hillside marking the successive shorelines.

Although much evidence has been found of Bronze Age settlement in Ennerdale, the valley seems to have remained relatively untouched by Roman and Norse invasions, though Gillerthwaite at the head of the lake, whose name is certainly of Norse origin, was a large cattle farm in the fourteenth century. Even with the rise in sheep farming on the monastic estates, the land at the head of Ennerdale remained forest as it was preserved for hunting and here the red deer were said in 1675 to be *as great as in any part of England.* A proposal in 1884 to build a railway up the wild and unspoilt valley was narrowly defeated in the House of Commons, the conservation lobby just managing to secure the necessary votes.

The twentieth century was to have the greatest effect ever wrought by man on Ennerdale, for in 1926 the Forestry Commission moved in. Planting of larch and spruce began almost immediately in one of the first commercially planted forests in Britain and with arithmetical precision trees soon covered the lower slopes. From Pillar and Scoat Fell to the south and on the northern side from Great Borne past Red Pike to Hay Stacks, straight-sided swathes of monotonous green covered the fellsides. Planting was so intensive that soil was imported so it could be extended to include steep rocky slopes. All

Black Sail Hut

those who loved Ennerdale were outraged and in 1935, when further forestry was planned in Eskdale and the Duddon valley, a petition was signed by 13,000 people which resulted the following year in an agreement to leave all the Central Fells unforested. The sacrifice of Ennerdale resulted in the saving of the heart of the Lake District.

After 1950 no further encroachment onto the fells was allowed and the first felling took place in 1979. Now the Ennerdale plantations are gradually becoming less harsh with the forest into its second rotation and the edges blurred to follow the contours of the valley. Different species such as Scots pine and native broadleaves are being planted, especially along the edge to create a more natural effect.

Ennerdale is nearly empty of habitation. There are just two youth hostels four miles apart and a field study centre. At the head of the valley beneath the slopes of Hay Stacks, is Black Sail Hut. This very basic youth hostel was once a shepherd's bothy and it is the most isolated hostel in England. Once nearly engulfed by the trees, considerable felling had taken place on our last visit and the forest boundaries had retreated to leave only truncated stumps by the hostel.

On the grass in front of the hut a walker studied his map, waiting for the hostel to open, while down by the River Liza a group was putting up its tents in the warm afternoon sunshine. But evening comes early to Ennerdale and as the shadows reached out down the valley we climbed on to enjoy another two hours of sun before it set behind Steeple as we put up our tent on the summit of Kirk Fell, once again on top of the world.

Pillar from High Crag

DAY 10 BLACK SAIL TO WASDALE HEAD

HIGH LEVEL ROUTE	Distance 9 miles	Ascent 3,300ft
(Wasdale	Distance 11 miles	Ascent 3,900ft)
LOW LEVEL ROUTE	Distance 3 miles	Ascent 900ft

ROUTE SUMMARY

High Level Route After climbing to Black Sail Pass the route lies over Pillar, Scoat Fell and Red Pike, then along the ridge of Yewbarrow and down to Wast Water. This is the Mosedale Horseshoe, a full and energetic day, one of the classics of the Lakes.

Low Level Route For those who spent the night at Black Sail Hut there is an easy crossing of Black Sail Pass down to Wasdale Head where the Wasdale Head Inn keeps its doors open all day.

Above Wasdale Head, beyond the hotel and the small enclosed fields fitting together like a jigsaw, is the quiet valley of Mosedale Beck. This is only one of the six Lakeland Mosedales, but it is so well-known, so famous, that the others seem mere pretenders to the name. Encircling the valley and forming a steep wall around its head is a ring of high mountains, Pillar, Black Crag, Scoat Fell and Red Pike, not one of them less than 2,500 feet. Here is the objective of those who come to seek out this Mosedale, the fells that link together to form one of the best horseshoe walks in the Lakes.

There are no half measures today. No starting out half-way round or missing out part of the walk in order to reach the evening's destination early. This is the full circuit, high above the valleys all day and with the long ridge of Yewbarrow as a fitting conclusion. Having said that, we must be honest and point out that there are some who claim Kirk Fell is part of the horseshoe, and even a few who like to include Great Gable, but whether you start from Black Sail Hut or Wasdale to climb to Black Sail Pass, the circuit of the Mosedale fells is a walk of which one never grows tired.

Yewbarrow, the lowest of the fells and only just above the 610m or 2,000-foot contour which entitles it to be called a mountain, has perhaps the best position. As you look up Wasdale towards the head of the lake, Great Gable is perfectly framed by the slopes of Sca Fell to the right and to the left by the shapely peak of Yewbarrow whose southern ridge sweeps down to the shore of Wast Water.

Much higher than Yewbarrow is Red Pike, a mere three miles distant from the Red Pike overlooking Buttermere, then higher still is Scoat Fell. But massive though it is and steep enough with crags shadowing its northern combes, Scoat Fell lacks the one essential ingredient of a proper mountain.

Yewbarrow and the head of Wast Water

It hasn't got a summit. True enough it has a cairn at about the highest point; in fact, on our last visit it had two, but there is no peak, no upthrust of rock to mark the highest point and along the long, level, grassy top processes a wall. Sitting uncomfortably on this wall, perched like Humpty Dumpty, is the summit cairn.

Better by far is Steeple. This is lower than Scoat Fell and linked to it by a narrow arête so closely that it cannot be anything other than a mere satellite, but it has a summit. A small, pointed, shapely summit with just enough room for a few people to stand together surrounded by the steep cliffs that plunge to the black combes of Mirk Cove and Mirklin Cove. No visit to the Mosedale fells would be complete without the out-and-back to Steeple.

The highest of all the Mosedale fells is Pillar, a massive bulk of a mountain, rising to 2,926 feet, and only a few feet lower than Great Gable. But it is not in the least like a pillar. The origins of its name remain a secret to those approaching from Wasdale until its extensive flat top is reached and you look down the northern slopes into Ennerdale. Those staying at Black Sail Hut will have seen it already. On the craggy northern face of Pillar, high above the dark green of the plantations and 500 feet from the screes at its foot to the small cairn on its very top, is Pillar Rock.

The first ascents of the Himalayan peaks, and the alpine ones too, are recent and recorded, but the first ascent of all the Lakeland peaks goes back into prehistory when man lived high above the valley swamps and the thick forest of the tree-covered hillsides. All that is, except Pillar Rock. Its vertical sides guarded the summit until 1826 when, on July 9, John Atkinson, an Ennerdale shepherd, climbed to the top by what is now called 'The Old West Route'. There were very few repetitions until the 1860s when rock climbing as a sport started to become popular in the district. In 1870 Miss A.Barker became the first lady to climb it and soon Pillar Rock was receiving the attentions of the rock climbing 'tigers'.

One of the early pioneers was not a tiger, but an endearing character called the Rev 'Steeple' Jackson, the vicar of Rivington near Bolton in Lancashire. He came to the fells late in life and acquired his nickname by climbing his own church steeple to repair the weathercock when no-one else could be found to do the job. Not one to eschew publicity, he was fond of composing verses about himself - a Mr Toad of the climbing world,

> *Who has not heard of Steeple Jack,*
> *That lion-hearted Saxon,*
> *Though I'm not he, he was my sire,*
> *For I am Steeple Jackson.*

He first climbed Pillar Rock in 1875 aged seventy-nine and the following year climbed it again solo. Two years later, when out walking in the winter, he slipped on the snow above Great Doup Cove and after a search his body was found at the foot of the crags. In his pocket was yet another verse.

We have a yellowing press cutting from 1971 describing the ascent of Pillar Rock by Colonel 'Rusty' Westmorland on his eighty-fifth birthday. He started young, with his first ascent in 1901 at the age of fifteen and in his later years celebrated by repeating the climb on his sixty-fifth, his seventy-fifth and lastly his eighty-fifth birthdays. Rusty, as he was universally known, founded the Keswick Mountain Rescue Team and was awarded the OBE in 1965 for his services to mountain rescue. This was the second mountain rescue team in the Lakes, the first being formed at Coniston by Jim Cameron.

Wainwright lovingly describes Pillar Rock in words and pictures, but it is a rock climb which he asserts is *positively out of bounds.* This was our last two-thousander in the Lakes, climbed on a hot July day when the rocks were warm to the touch and alpine flowers bloomed beside the path. We had left it till last, not because it was difficult, but because it was the last summit in England and Wales to be attained by man and, it seemed fitting that it should be our last summit too.

Afterwards, pausing frequently to look back, we climbed the steep slopes to the summit of Pillar mountain where we sat by the cairn and eagerly opened our packed lunch. It was white sliced bread, a disappointment in itself, but worse still, it was filled with plentiful helpings of onion. A sheep approached expectantly, we offered it the onion and to our surprise it scoffed the lot and came back for more. If anyone that day met a sheep on Pillar with unusually bad breath, you now know why!

Many a time we have descended Scoat Fell towards Red Pike and stopped for a drink at the ice-cold spring that rises from the mosses on its slopes. One day we said, we would come and camp on these fells and what a good water supply it would be. In the autumn of 1990 having pitched our tent on the flat summit of Scoat Fell we came down nonchalantly to collect the water. The spring was almost dry. This was the first time it had been anything other than a torrent, and it was with great difficulty that we managed to coax a trickle sufficient for our meal. But it was a perfect spot to spend the night with a view to delight any fellwalker's heart. From our tent doorway we looked across at Steeple's bare cone of rock and watched the sun sink into the still waters of the Solway Firth. Then after a calm, starlit night we rose just before dawn to see the orange disc of the sun gradually appear on Gable's shoulder.

ROUTE DESCRIPTION
If the night was spent in luxury at Wasdale Head the High Level Route is joined at the summit of Black Sail Pass by following today's Low Level Route in reverse.

JOINT ROUTE
On leaving **Black Sail Hut** head towards the hills with Great Gable high above at the head of the valley, but just beyond the end of the forest turn off right over the footbridge to climb beside Sail Beck on a clear path up Black Sail Pass, an old packhorse way. On the grassy slopes there is a profusion of alpine lady's mantle with its lupin-like leaves, which we have seen in flower as late as September. It is a climb of 800 feet before **Black Sail Pass Summit** is reached, a welcome but momentary respite, with a view beyond down into Mosedale. Ahead the skyline is all of mountains, Yewbarrow, Red Pike, and Scoat Fell, though the summit of Pillar is still out of sight.

HIGH LEVEL ROUTE
Following the well-trodden path along the ridge, the minor summit of **Looking Stead,** may be omitted, but it is worth a few minutes detour to follow the fence up to the cairn from which the head of Ennerdale can be surveyed. Looking down the valley, on the northern slope of Pillar is Robinson's cairn which marks the end of the high level traverse to Pillar Rock and far below a green tide of trees laps against the mountains. While the Forestry Commission is making valiant attempts to blend its conifers into the landscape, and by selective felling replacing the mathematically precise straight edge of the original plantation with carefully designed curves, the dark green mass is still an intrusion into the valley.

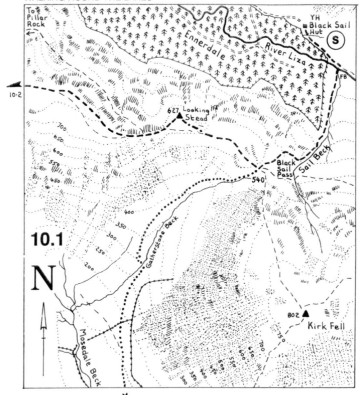

Returning to the path the ascent begins again and just after the col the small cairn which marks the start of the high-level traverse is passed. A clear, rocky path climbs easily westwards up the ridge and to the left far below is the hamlet of Wasdale Head. Near the top on the right is Great Doup Cove where the Rev Steeple Jackson fell to his death in 1882, then the fence posts act as a guide in mist over the last short section to the summit.

While **Pillar** is one of the Lakeland giants, its summit is rather tame, a flat expanse of stone and grass with a wind shelter, a trig point, a couple of begging sheep, and not much else. But a few steps to the north and one looks down on Pillar Rock, the only two-thousand-foot summit in the whole of England and Wales which requires rock climbing skills to reach it. Down the valley Ennerdale Water shines silver and on the horizon is the Solway Firth,

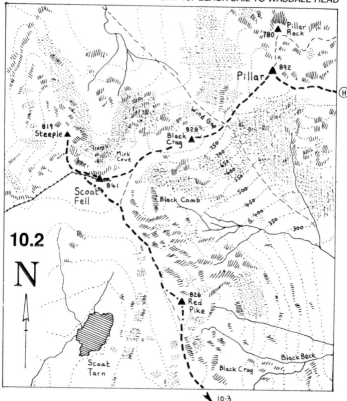

10.2

N

then to the north beyond the intervening ridge of High Crag and High Stile are the pink screes of Grasmoor, the highest of the North-Western Fells. The north-eastern horizon is of Skiddaw and Blencathra, eastwards is the full length of the Helvellyn range, and to the south-east are the Scafells with the massive shape of Great Gable in the foreground rising above Kirk Fell.

From Pillar the route lies south-west following a line of cairns down over easy rocks to **Wind Gap**, which like Windy Gap between Green Gable and Great Gable, is a natural wind tunnel. The vertiginous scree shoot to the left provides an escape route into the head of Mosedale in bad weather. A steep ascent with a scrambling finish brings you to **Black Crag** and though a cairn marks the summit, there is another a little beyond, more comfortable as a perch from which to take in the panorama of mountains.

Steeple

After a pleasant grassy stroll above the scalloped rim of the gullies, Scoat Fell is the next top which is reached with little effort up a stony path to tumbled boulders. But where is the top? A stone wall follows the ridge for mile after mile into the distance and while one might suppose that Great Scoat Fell was the highest, in fact Little Scoat Fell is pre-eminent. The cairn sits atop the wall, but the summit of **Scoat Fell** is unremarkable, so flat that a precise top is difficult to locate and in fact so flat we camped very comfortably on it one night.

Steeple is connected to Scoat Fell by a narrow rib of rock, and although it is an out-and-back, no circuit of the Mosedale Horseshoe would be complete without including the brief ascent to its splendid top. Follow the wall to the corner where a little cairned path makes a diversion of only a few minutes to visit the summit, a small platform which is a fine belvedere high above Ennerdale from which to see the cliffs of Mirk Cove and Black Crag.

Return to the wall corner and head south-east, avoiding the rocks and by-passing the summit of Scoat Fell, down to a grassy col. The next summit **Red Pike** is not, like its namesake in Buttermere, coloured red. The main

150

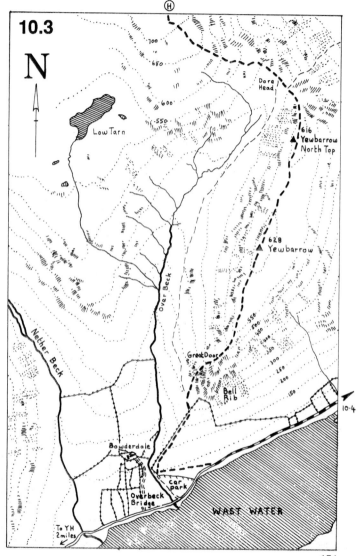

path perversely misses the top and must be quitted to visit the cairn perched on the very edge of the drop into Mosedale on the furthest rocky point.

Following the ridge, rejoin the main path to Yewbarrow, the final summit of the day. When seen from Wasdale, Yewbarrow apparently towers over all the other fells, a veritable giant, but as one starts to descend towards Dore Head it looks a very minor fell and hardly worth the effort. Then as the descent continues, and it seems to go on for a long time, Yewbarrow gradually resumes its stature, the rocks ahead appearing quite formidable. At **Dore Head** a small path to the right above Over Beck can be taken to avoid the fell altogether, and there is also an alternative finish down the uninviting Dorehead Screes to Wasdale Head, but the way up is a lot easier than it looks, a well-worn scramble through the rocks. On reaching the grassy ridge the northern summit is a little way along it, to the right of the path.

Strolling easily south for half a mile, the main top of **Yewbarrow** is reached with its little cairn. Across the head of Wasdale lie tomorrow's routes, the Low Level passing Burnmoor Tarn and the High Level climbing to Scafell Pike and Sca Fell.

It is a gentle descent along the ridge with Wast Water beneath your feet until the rocks at Great Door are met. Ahead is Bell Rib and while the ridge path continues to the very brink this is only for rock climbers and the steep loose scree shoot on the right must be taken instead. At first progress feels safest to the right, but in the lower part the left-hand side is to be preferred. Joining the path this brings you to a ladder stile and thence down by the wall to Overbeck Bridge. **Wasdale Head** lies 1½ miles up the road to the left, but **Wastwater Youth Hostel** is a 2½ miles tramp along the lakeside road in the other direction.

LOW LEVEL ROUTE

After descending at first steeply from **Black Sail Pass summit,** the angle soon eases and the bridleway keeps above Gatherstone Beck before zigzagging down to ford the stream. The bridge that spanned the beck at this point when the packhorse route was in regular use has long disappeared. The track descends gently, curving round to the left into Mosedale through a little gate by a stile to meet Mosedale Beck just before it vanishes over Ritson's Force. This was named in honour of Will Ritson, the first landlord of the Wasdale Head Inn, who proudly claimed to be England's biggest liar. The track then climbs a little to another gate and stile before rounding the corner where the hamlet of **Wasdale Head** appears below. Continue to follow the beck down, past the little packhorse bridge to the Wasdale Head Inn and its ever-open bar.

WASDALE

The tiny hamlet of Wasdale Head, a handful of farms, a church and a hotel,

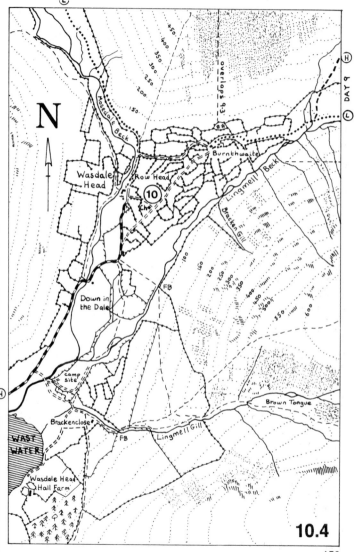

10.4

is set in a patchwork of stone-walled fields that fill the end of valley. The walls, several feet thick in places, speak of the tireless labour which cleared the little fields. Surplus stones are piled into huge mounds and although many of the walls over the fells have been built within the last two hundred years, the clearance of the Wasdale land started around 800 years ago. There was still a common field at Wasdale Head in the early sixteenth century, but the enclosures at Wasdale and in many of the surrounding valleys were virtually complete by the early 1600s.

Wasdale Head is said to have the deepest lake, the highest mountain, the smallest church and the biggest liar in England. While the claim to the smallest church is disputed, for although it is the smallest in Cumbria there are a few elsewhere in England which are even smaller, the other superlatives can be verified. Of Scafell Pike there can be no doubt or of Wast Water, too, which is 258 feet deep with a bed 58 feet below sea level, while Will Ritson was a legend in his own lifetime.

In the 1850s Wasdale Head, after many centuries of quiet seclusion, was invaded by climbers. In those days it was only the relatively well-off who made the long journey to this remote valley, but it became popular enough for Will Ritson to obtain a licence for his farmhouse at Rowfoot in 1856 and turn it into the Huntsman's Inn. He was the landlord until 1879 and built the first of the extensions to the original farmhouse. Born in 1808 he lived all his life in the valley and was a champion wrestler, a competent fell guide and a teller of tall stories and at the local shows he was declared "the greatest liar in England". One oft-recounted story tells of when he took a visiting bishop up Sca Fell. On reaching the summit he turned to his client saying: *Well, here ye are Mr Bishop, as near to heaven as ye ever will be.* The story-telling tradition continues today as since 1974 the 'Biggest Liar in the World' competition has been held annually at Santon Bridge.

The tiny church, set a little apart across the fields and surrounded by yew trees, was originally a chapel of Saint Bees Priory, but after it became a parish church it was dedicated in 1979 to the Norse Saint Olaf. It has within its parish boundary just four farmhouses and the hotel. Tradition says the ancient church building was first constructed from Viking longboat timbers and the present building dates from at least the sixteenth century. In a corner of the churchyard a few simple headstones mark the graves of climbers and in the south window is an engraving of Napes Needle and the opening words of Psalm 121:

> *I will lift up mine eyes unto the hills,*
> *from whence cometh my strength.*

Beside the inn is an outdoor pursuits shop which has a fair range of gear and also a limited amount of food; there is a tree-screened National Trust campsite by the head of the lake and all the farms do bed and breakfast. It was once a simple climbers' hotel where extra guests slept on the billiard room table or in the bath, there was no 'en suite' then!

Wastwater Youth Hostel is a four-mile hike down the road. Standing in its own extensive grounds beside the lake, Wasdale Hall was built in 1929 and is now owned by the National Trust. In a ghostly tale the grounds are reputed to be haunted by the mother of a child who was drowned in the lake in the 1820s.

Electricity came very late to Wasdale Head as for many years the understandable wishes of the inhabitants were opposed by conservationists who refused, equally understandably, to allow overhead cables to spoil the valley. The eventual solution was a cable, which was laid along the bed of the lake in 1977.

West Water like Buttermere and Ennerdale Water is a very pure lake, so pure, in fact, that virtually nothing grows in it, as what little lime and other bases there are in the rocks have been leached from their surface by ten thousand years of Lake District rain. Boating is not allowed on the lake, only the occasional wet-suited windsurfer tacks to and fro on the wild dark waters of the lake overlooked by the grandest mountains in Lakeland.

Packhorse bridge, Wasdale Head   155

Scafell Pike from Three Tarns

DAY 11 WASDALE HEAD TO ESKDALE

HIGH LEVEL ROUTE	Distance 9 miles	Ascent 4,000ft
LOW LEVEL ROUTE	Distance 7½ miles	Ascent 750ft

ROUTE SUMMARY

High Level Route The most strenuous day of the tour which, after climbing Scafell Pike, the highest point in England, drops to Mickledore and then ascends Sca Fell by Foxes Tarn. The bouldery tops are hard going but are followed by an easy walk down over the little-frequented Slight Side into Eskdale.

Low Level Route Skirting Sca Fell, an old corpse road leads past Burnmoor Tarn to Boot with a visit to a corn-mill and, if there is time, a trip on 'Little Ratty'.

Attracting a constant stream of visitors from morning to evening, the summit of Scafell Pike was as usual busy, with crowds round the cairn, but ignored and as though invisible to everyone else, we pitched our tent a short way below it one July afternoon. It was still early, but the promise of fine weather had tempted us to spend the night on England's highest summit.

We sat in the feeble sunshine of the late afternoon that shone through gradually dispersing cloud. Northwards, Gable, Pillar, Kirk Fell, all seemed far away and strangely diminished, while in the low flat grassy ridge below us we failed momentarily to recognise the mighty Yewbarrow. The blue familiar outlines of Skiddaw and Blencathra filled the northern view and on the eastern horizon the long, high ridge stretched from Clough Head over Helvellyn to Fairfield and its satellites, with the characteristic dip in the skyline that identifies Grisedale Tarn. Each summit of the Coniston fells was recited with the pleasure of remembered days among them, while to the south the view was of Sca Fell, its massive presence cutting off all beyond and challenging the supremacy of Scafell Pike.

Gradually the crowds dwindled until the summit was deserted, but then two groups approached, one from Borrowdale, one from Wasdale. They met and stopped just below where we sat on the cairn. "We're doing the three peaks", one group announced, "Ben Nevis, Scafell Pike and Snowdon in twenty-four hours". The others looked surprised. "So are we," they chorused. Taking photos of each other they looked briefly at the view before setting off smartly downhill, but soon more people appeared, once more from opposite directions. Again the same announcement was made and again it received the same reply, one group was even attempting a rock climb on all three summits. But Ben Nevis, Snowdon and Scafell Pike are so widely separated

157

that long hours must be spent in the car if the task is to be completed within the standard time and we were content to sit there watching the sun sink behind the veil of cloud on the horizon as they all departed to leave us once again alone. That night we were the highest people in the whole of England.

Crowning the summit of Scafell Pike is a massive circular cairn about five feet high, flat on top and with a small flight of steps on one side which permits walkers to climb to the very highest point in England. On the cairn is a plaque:

> *In perpetual memory of the men of the Lake District who fell for God and King, for Freedom, Peace and Right in the Great War 1914-1918. This summit of Scafell was given to the nation subject to any commoners rights and placed in custody of the National Trust by Charles Henry Baron Leconfield 1919.*

After a first glance, you read it again: "this summit of Scafell". But surely we are on Scafell Pike? In fact Scafell Pike has only comparatively recently been recognised as the highest. For many years it was nameless or referred to simply as "The Pikes" and certainly when seen from most viewpoints it is difficult to credit that Sca Fell is not the higher as it appears to overtop its companion. But the Ordnance Survey, though the occasional error does from time to time creep into its almost perfect cartography, has not made a mistake. Though its height has varied with the increasing precision of surveys from 3,210 feet in Wainwright's day to 3,206 feet and finally to 978 metres, Scafell Pike reigns supreme.

Dorothy Wordsworth was familiar with this problem and in Wordsworth's *Guide to the Lakes* describes their "Excursion to the top of Scawfell":

> *We saw the summit of Scaw-fell, apparently very near to us; and we shaped our course towards it; but, discovering that it could not be reached without first making a considerable descent, we resolved, instead, to aim at another point of the same mountain, called the 'Pikes', which I have since found has been estimated as higher than the summit bearing the name of Scawfell Head, where the Stone Man is built.*

The Wordsworths were very lucky with the weather on their visit in 1818 for Dorothy goes on:

> *The sun had never once been overshadowed by a cloud during the whole of our progress from the centre of Borrowdale. On the summit of the Pike, which we gained after much toil, though without difficulty, there was not a breath of air to stir even the papers containing our refreshment, as they lay spread out upon a rock. The stillness seemed to be not of this world: we paused, and kept silence to listen; and no sound could be heard: the Scawfell Cataracts were voiceless to us; and there was not an insect to hum in the air. The vales which*

we had seen from Ash-course lay yet in view; and, side by side with Eskdale, we now saw the sister Vale of Donnerdale terminated by the Duddon Sands. But the majesty of the mountains below, and close to us, is not to be conceived. We now beheld the whole mass of Great Gavel from its base, the Den of Wastdale at our feet a gulph immeasurable: Grasmire and the other mountains of Crummock - Ennerdale and its mountains; and the Sea beyond!

Separating Sca Fell from Scafell Pike is Mickledore, a great gash in the skyline which instantly identifies the mountain's silhouette. Ahead is an impasse. There are three commonly used ways between Scafell Pike and Sca Fell. To the right is Lord's Rake, a steep slippery scree shoot, the foot of which necessitates an initial descent towards Hollow Stones; to the left is the Foxes Tarn route, which again necessitates a descent; while straight ahead is Broad Stand. Go and look at Broad Stand by all means; it starts with a narrow slit at the foot of the face, known as Fat Man's Agony, but this leads to an awkward and exposed move with more difficulties above. It is a rock climb.

The first descent of Broad Stand is credited to Samuel Taylor Coleridge while he was on a walking tour in 1802 and though it is possible that he actually climbed down Scafell Chimney, the cleft next to Broad Stand, his description fits the series of ledges above Mickledore, where having *skirted the precipices* he dropped down from ledge to ledge:

So I began to suspect, that I ought not to go on, but then unfortunately tho' I could with ease drop down a smooth rock 7 feet high, I could not climb it, so go on I must, and on I went, the next 3 drops were not half a Foot, at least not a foot more than my own height, but every Drop increased the Palsy of my limbs I shook all over, Heaven knows without the least influence of Fear, and now I had only two more to drop down, to return was impossible.

After having a rest on his back and after encountering a very dead sheep, Coleridge made it safely down to the ridge, surviving to recall the episode in a letter, not to his wife, but to Sara Hutchinson, Wordsworth's sister-in-law which he had started on the summit of Sca Fell: *Surely the first Letter ever written from the Top of Sca' Fell!*

A few weeks after our camp on the summit we were again climbing Scafell Pike, this time sauntering up with a group of friends and carrying only day sacks, when Anne received an encouraging kindly pat on the shoulder from a fell runner as he jogged past. "You're doing all right, love," he said, "I think you'll make it!"

ROUTE DESCRIPTION

JOINT ROUTE

Leaving **Wasdale Head** walk down its only road to the bend, past the little green and the school. Like the nearby vicarage, this was built in 1888 but the numbers of local children declined until it finally closed in 1913 and now its sole use is to store the hurdles for the Wasdale Show. The right-most path leads through the fields towards the lake, though if the bridleway is flooded the river crossing can be avoided by continuing down the road to the National Trust campsite. Crossing two small streams and a large, stony, but usually dry, river channel, the campsite is reached with its all-year-round exhibition of lightweight tents. After 100 yards a gate on the left leads out to the main track and across Lingmell Gill, where the distant crags of Scafell Pike can be seen framed between Lingmell and Sca Fell. Fork left signed 'Eskdale and Scafells Route', then just before **Brackenclose**, which has belonged to the Fell and Rock Climbing Club since 1937, the High and Low Routes part company.

HIGH LEVEL ROUTE

The path to the Scafells keeps beside Lingmell Gill, crossing it at a footbridge, and then climbs the bracken-covered slopes beside the gill before recrossing higher up. This is the **Brown Tongue** route, both the shortest and the easiest way up England's highest mountain. Plodding steadily up the stony track with the long ridge of Lingmell to the left and Black Crag to the right, we paused for a chat with two National Trust workers busy 'pitching' the path. Already the lower section was blending into its surroundings and was much more attractive than the former torn turf and scree, but progress is slow and it would be many months before their work was finished. After a climb of 1,500 feet the angle eases and Hollow Stones is reached. Here beneath the crags is an oasis of grass and bilberry among the rocks and boulders. Ahead is Pike's Crag and Pulpit Rock, one of the finest crags of Scafell Pike, and to the right, perhaps playing hide-and-seek in the swirling cloud, are the massive rock buttresses of Sca Fell. A broad scree shoot runs up to the notch in the skyline which is Mickledore where tiny figures outlined on the col give scale to the massive surrounding cliffs, but ignoring this slithery scramble take instead the faint, but cairned path which climbs easily north-east towards **Lingmell Col**, the dip in the skyline.

As the col is reached the path bends right, but for the energetic an out-and-back to Lingmell summit adds less than half an hour to the expedition and from its top there is a breathtaking view down into Piers Gill directly below. These cliffs are among half a dozen favoured spots in the Lake District where on ledges out of reach of the sheep and supplied with minerals continually leached from the rocks, flowers long disappeared from the rest of the fells cling on.

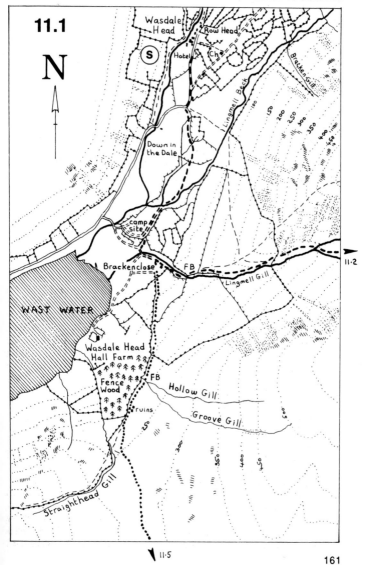

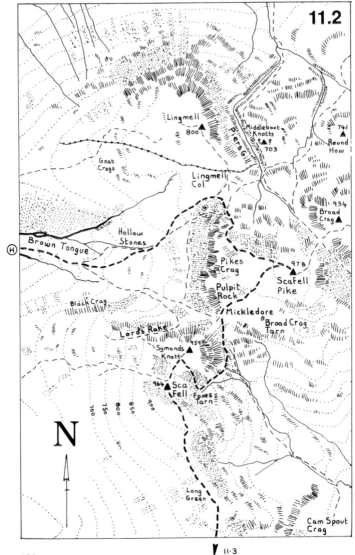

11.2

Lingmell
▲ 800

Peers G'

Middleboot Knotts
▲ ▲ 703

741 ▲
Round How

Goat Crags

Lingmell Col

934 ▲
Broad Crag ▲

Hollow Stones

Brown Tongue

ⓗ

Pikes Crag

978 ▲
Scafell Pike

Pulpit Rock

Black Crag

Mickledore

Broad Crag Tarn

Lords Rake

▲ 959
Symonds Knott

964 ▲ Sca Fell
Foxes Tarn

100
150
800
850
900

N

Long Green

Cam Spout Crag

↓ 11·3

Climbing southwards from Lingmell Col on the broad stony path up the north-western ridge of Scafell Pike, the pink-streaked rocks and screes of Great Gable's southern face appear almost precipitous. It is an easy ascent of 750 feet to the flat area just below the top of **Scafell Pike** where a few patches of grass and moss grow among the stones, but the summit rising above its surroundings is all of boulders. Following the cairns, pick your way over the stony waste to the highest point whose massive circular platform dwarfing the OS trig point has a commemorative tablet. The plaque was brought to the summit in a wheelbarrow and built into the cairn by the men of the Ordnance Survey when they were constructing their trig point. In 1987 the cairn was repaired by the National Trust.

There is a multiplicity of windshelters on the inhospitable top, one of which is quite substantial with the remains of a fireplace, a flagged floor and a raised bench. If you are lucky enough to have clear weather the views are truly magnificent, though for many days of the year the top is shrouded in mist and you can only read frustratingly of what you would be able to see if you could. To the south and usually quite deserted is the little peak of Scafell Pike's subsidiary summit and beyond, some seven miles away, are the Coniston fells. Closer at hand are Bow Fell and the Langdale Pikes, to the north-east are Broad Crag and Ill Crag, two satellites of Scafell Pike both topping 3,000 feet, and on the far eastern horizon is the Helvellyn range. Northwards are Blencathra and Skiddaw and above the vertical screes of Great Gable rise Grasmoor and the North-Western Fells. The bulk of Sca Fell fills the view to the south-west and just visible beyond its dramatic cliffs, Wast Water stretches out towards the sea and the blue silhouette of the Isle of Man.

Retracing your steps, descend north-west from the trig point to the flat bouldery shelf, then fork left on the well-cairned path heading south-west towards Sca Fell. Take care in mist or you may, as we once did, find yourself back at the Lingmell Col. The rough and stony path leads down to **Mickledore** and ahead are the overhanging cliffs of Scafell Crag, often with the tiny figures of climbers high on the face. To the left on a grassy shelf below the stones is Broad Crag Tarn, the highest tarn in the Lake District. At the col is a stretcher box while straight ahead is Broad Stand, for climbers only.

A few yards beyond the stretcher box a narrow trod slants left across the rough screes then descends beneath the cliffs. It feels much further down than you think it ought to be, but eventually the path reaches an obvious gully.

For an escape route in bad weather, continue descending to reach the River Esk and follow it for 1½ miles down to Lingcove Bridge where map 12.2 shows the route down Eskdale.

A rather damp scramble up rocks, bright in summer with the starry saxifrage, leads to the tiny pool of **Foxes Tarn**, the second highest tarn in the Lake District. The next bit is scree, a loose, tiring scree with two steps up and

163

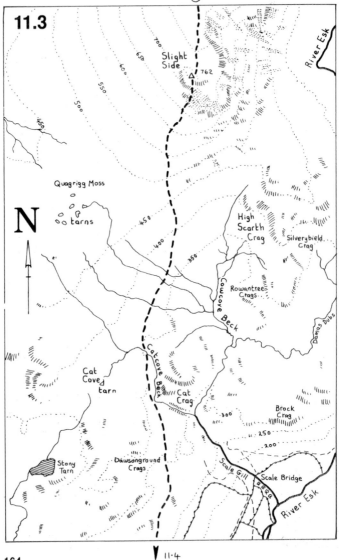

Sca Fell and Hollow Stones

one down, but easier in ascent than descent and eventually the path emerges at a grassy col between the two summits of Sca Fell. To the right is the lower summit of **Symonds Knott**, a massive heap of awkward boulders named after the Rev H.H.Symonds, founder of the Friends of the Lake District. With more than 50 feet of ascent from the col this rates as a separate top and can easily be ticked off en route by peak baggers. Further right is Deep Gill and the Pinnacle, where from the safety of the path which leads round the edge, the rock face can be seen falling sheer into the depths of the gully which is crossed in its lower reaches by Lord's Rake.

From the grassy col a line of cairns leads south-west to the summit cairn of **Sca Fell** with its nearby wind shelter. Although to the north-east the hills are hidden by the bulk of Scafell Pike where little stick men stand on the summit platform, in the opposite direction the view stretches all the way to the sea.

Making your way south along the stony ridge the going becomes easier. Below to the right is the silver sheen of Burnmoor Tarn and beyond the tarn is the hidden head of Miterdale which is thought to have been Arthur

165

Ransome's "little secret valley of Swallowdale". After descending more screes, the edge of the cliffs is followed to Long Green and at the far end of the ridge a cairn marks a little rise which gives a final view of Mickledore and the Scafells. The path continues, now easily and mainly on grass to the rocky top of **Slight Side**, with a little scramble to the highest point. This is a good spot from which to study tomorrow's route up Eskdale to Bow Fell and the Crinkles.

Continue to descend with at first yet more slippery scree and then with relief over grassy slopes to a large cairned boulder where the path swings right high above the boggy valley of Cowcove Beck. The little path wanders on by rocky knolls till nearing the road you can look down on Eskdale and pick out Hardknott Fort on the slopes beyond and Hardknott Pass, one of the most difficult roads in Great Britain with a gradient of one in three. Finally after following above a wall the road is reached where you turn right to Boot and **Eskdale Youth Hostel**.

LOW LEVEL ROUTE

At **Brackenclose** take the bridleway signed 'Eskdale' and passing the climbing hut, go through the gate. The path slants across the hillside climbing steadily following the wall beside Fence Wood past a row of tumbledown cottages. This was the route by which corpses were taken from Wasdale for interment at Saint Catherine's in Boot before the little church at Wasdale Head was consecrated in 1901. Forking left towards Burnmoor Tarn, the Scafells may well be shrouded in mist, but as you climb the views of Wast Water expand while Yewbarrow towers over the lake apparently rivalling the giants at the head of the dale. From this angle Great Gable with its pink-streaked scree hides shyly behind Lingmell, Kirk Fell rises in steep unbroken

The Pinnacle, Sca Fell

slopes and beyond the summit of Pillar can just be seen. The cairned path climbs gradually to the flat col with Sca Fell to the left presenting an uncharacteristically grassy backside, while to the right Illgill Head, the end of the Wast Water Screes, looks unremittingly steep.

Reaching the highest point near the ancient cairn of Maiden Castle, **Burnmoor Tarn** appears ahead with Burnmoor Lodge, a former hunting lodge, on the far side. This whole area, which has many Bronze Age settlements, was covered in oak woods when the Romans came. The path then skirts the stony edge of the tarn, a surprisingly large stretch of water, quiet and peaceful but slightly gloomy. Past the tarn the track divides into three. Keeping straight on, the grassy path climbs gently to the right of Whillan Beck, with Harter Fell ahead and Grey Friar in the background. The cairned path is rather indistinct until the track from the lodge is joined. Then it descends through a series of gates and past the original site of the railway station below an old iron mine. This was the Nab Gill Mine. Never very prosperous, it was worked from the middle of the nineteenth century intermittently until 1917 when it was finally abandoned. Continue down the track to the corn-mill and over the packhorse bridge into **Boot**.

BOOT

The tiny village of Boot with its stone walls of pink Eskdale granite and whitewashed cottages was once a thriving mining and farming community. As you descend to the village, above Gill Bank Farm and on the opposite side of Whillan Beck there was a carding mill and beside the packhorse bridge is Eskdale Mill, a water-powered corn-mill which was in operation from the sixteenth century until 1920. The corn-mill, restored by the county planning committee in 1975 and opened to visitors the following year, has a grain drying loft and was powered by an overshot wheel. In the centre of the village is the Burnmoor Inn, the Fold End Gallery and a post office which sells a rudimentary amount of provisions, but though the village is small enough, neither its church nor its railway station are close at hand.

Relaxing in the warm sunshine with a cream tea outside Brook House we learned that it was the seventy-fifth anniversary of the Ravenglass and Eskdale Railway. Hurrying down to the station we were in time to see one of the trains arrive with the staff in period costumes and the driver wearing a red neckerchief and black top hat. Dalegarth station is the terminus for 'Little Ratty', the narrow gauge railway from Ravenglass. It is open all year and the scenic seven-mile journey to the coast takes about forty minutes.

The railway was started in 1875 to carry ore from the Nab Gill iron mine, and also slate from the local quarries, to the main railway. After a hesitant beginning, and although it became a major tourist attraction, it was uneconomical and closed in 1913. In 1915 the line was converted to a fifteen inch narrow gauge and in this form served the nearby Beckfoot granite quarry

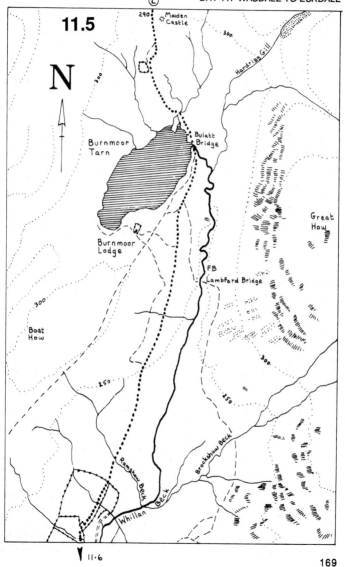

11.5

N

290 Maiden Castle

300

Hardrigg Gill

Burnmoor Tarn

300

Bulatt Bridge

Great How

Burnmoor Lodge

FB
Lambford Bridge

300

Boat How

300

250

250

Ramshaw Beck

Brockshaw Beck

Whillan Beck

▼ 11·6

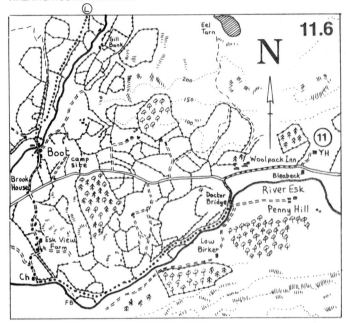

until, with the quarry, it shut again in 1953. The railway was saved at an auction in 1960 by a band of local enthusiasts. The present Dalegarth terminus was built in 1926, and before that the line extended past the village to mines higher up the valley which were worked from 1870 to 1884. A section of this old trackbed is passed if you follow the riverside path to the youth hostel.

At the end of a stony lane and on the banks of the River Esk, Saint Catherine's Church dates from the fourteenth century and the time when the Furness monks owned the land around Eskdale, although the present building is only a little over a hundred years old. An interesting feature in the churchyard is Tommy Dobson's grave. Founder of the Eskdale and Ennerdale Farmer's Hunt in 1857 and Master of it for fifty-three years, he died in 1910 aged eighty-three. His unusual carved gravestone depicts a huntsman with a fox and hounds. When we visited the church in late summer the porch was busy, but not with the comings and goings of the congregation. A barn swallow had built her nest inside the porch and fearlessly swooped in and out to feed her young who waited, appropriately dressed in white bibs and black dog collars.

Eskdale Youth Hostel

ROUTE TO ESKDALE YOUTH HOSTEL

Passing the Burnmoor Inn and a gallery, go down to the road junction. The youth hostel is a good mile up the road to the left, but a much prettier alternative is to take the walled track opposite Brook House which leads to Saint Catherine's Church, and follow the footpath beside the River Esk to Doctor Bridge. Turn left at the bridge and then right along the road past the Woolpack Inn to **Eskdale Youth Hostel**.

ESKDALE

Purpose-built rather than adapted from some previous building, Eskdale Youth Hostel is just over a mile east of the village of Boot, perhaps a little too far for an evening stroll after dinner, but fortunately close to the Woolpack Inn. The inn was built in this isolated spot specially to serve the packhorse trains carrying loads of wool to Whitehaven as they descended from Hardknott and Wrynose or came from Coniston via Walna Scar and Harter Fell. Penny Hill on the opposite bank of the River Esk and on the original packhorse track was once a rival inn reached via Doctor Bridge, named after Dr Edward Tyson of Penny Hill who widened it in 1734.

The River Esk, which is born on the slopes of Esk Hause to the west of Bow Fell flows down to meet the sea at Ravenglass and beside the estuary are the remains of a Roman Fort, Glanoventa. The road from this fort to the one at Ambleside passed over Hardknott Pass and overlooking the Eskdale valley in a strategically commanding position, the Romans built the fort of

171

Mediobogdum.

Hardknott Fort was constructed early in the second century, in the reign of the emperor Hadrian between 117 and 138AD. About 1½ miles from the youth hostel and standing on a shelf by the side of the pass, it is very impressive with three-feet high walls enclosing a large area with a tower at each corner. The gateway in each wall has pillars of red sandstone which was quarried some distance away at Gosforth and inside the walls are the remains of various buildings including the commandant's house. A little way down the hillside towards the road and outside the walls is the bath house.

Although the hillside is now bare, and nowadays just a sea of grass, in Roman times it would all have been covered with trees so the Roman soldiers had first to clear the area to build the fort and the extensive parade ground. The parade ground is large, about three acres, and big enough for as many as 600 soldiers to assemble and drill there. The hillside has been artificially levelled to provide this platform above the fort and at one side is a raised mound on which the drill sergeant perhaps bellowed his orders. The fort was probably abandoned early in the third century and its ruins look down on the cars which every summer struggle over the hairpin bends of the Hardknott Pass.

'RIVER IRT', Ravenglass and Eskdale Railway

Bow Fell from Three Tarns

DAY 12 BOOT TO GREAT LANGDALE

HIGH LEVEL ROUTE   Distance 11 miles   Ascent 3,500ft
LOW LEVEL ROUTE   Distance 8 miles   Ascent 2,100ft

ROUTE SUMMARY

For the first few miles both the High and Low Routes take a common course following the lovely River Esk up into the hills to Lingcove Bridge. Continuing beside Lingcove Beck, the ways divide below Bow Fell.

High Level Route Heading for Ore Gap and then over Bow Fell, the route continues along the delightful switchback ridge of Crinkle Crags before descending by way of Red Tarn to Langdale. While the approach is easy and fast, the ridge is rough and progress is slower over the tops

Low Level Route Diverging below Bow Fell the route climbs to the col at Three Tarns and thence down The Band on a good path to Langdale. NOTE: The two routes cross at Three Tarns, so second thoughts allow the alternative to be joined.

Almost as soon as you leave the road to follow the River Esk upstream, the shapely cone of Bow Fell comes into view, four miles distant at the head of the valley. Bow Fell is nearly, though not quite, a three-thousander, but while the first glimpse of the mountain is impressive, a massive pointed pyramid rising above the surrounding fells, its true size only becomes apparent when after a full mile of walking it does not seem to be any closer . The southern face, which Bow Fell turns to this approach, is furrowed with scree-filled gullies known as Bowfell Links and on its northern side the steep cliffs of Hanging Knotts drop to the ice-scoured hollow of Angle Tarn. From the eastern side Bow Fell is equally impressive, with massive buttresses of rock, Cambridge Crag, Bowfell Buttress and Flat Crags looking down on Great Langdale. The summit of Bow Fell is boulders, a great pile of them heaped in a pyramid over and around which the pilgrims scramble, for it is a mecca to which its devotees return again and again.

A cold clear December morning saw us climbing out of the dark shadows of the valley, not as yet touched by the sun which lit the mountain above. The beck was skimmed with ice, the ground was frozen hard and waterfalls had slowed to a trickle with huge icicles hanging like silver organ pipes from the rocks. The air was cold, below freezing, but so still that as soon as we came into the warmth of the sunlight, gloves, hats and anoraks were rapidly discarded. As we climbed towards the skyline ahead, we passed into the shadow of the upper rocks, the cold began to seep through and we quickened our pace. Once again we came into the sunlight, but now around
174

Bow Fell and Crinkle Crags looking up Eskdale

us was a world of white; not snow, but hoar frost, shining crystals that covered the rocks and stones and glistened and sparkled in the sun. To the south the Coniston fells looked far away and hard to see as we screwed up our eyes against the glare of the sun.

There were only a few figures on the summit; it had been an early start and while we religiously touched the cairn to formally register another ascent, our eyes were on the Scafells. With a foreground of hoar frost crystal and the more distant golden yellow of the winter grass, the mountains across the head of Eskdale stood clear and sharply outlined. Sca Fell and Scafell Pike, separated by the chasm of Mickledore, rose from impenetrable black shadows. Above a raven called.

Ice, frost and snow are here not only in the winter months and one April afternoon we picked our way along Crinkle Crags which looked strangely unfamiliar under the steadily falling snow. The "Bad Step", a short but vertical rock wall, seemed harder than usual with heavy packs and holds covered in wet snow so we followed the easier but circuitous path up to Long Top. We reached the cairn and continued along the ridge. There was no sign of a path, the snow covered everything, but we had been here many times; there was no need even to look at the map. Gradually we descended, seeking the little tarn where we had planned to pitch our mountain tent. But where was it?

175

There were signs of a path, but soon we began to doubt; surely there wasn't this much descent on the ridge? The map and compass told all. North lay the ridge, but we were heading west along the spine of Long Top and going down steeply and rapidly towards Eskdale. In the failing light we retraced our steps to the cairn and this time, taking a careful bearing, continued along the ridge. Our chosen tarn proved elusive, frozen and completely covered in snow, but soon the tent was up beside its grey shape and we had our home for the night.

The approach from Eskdale up the long valley of the River Esk is one of gradually increasing interest. The lower part of the valley is wide, with stone-walled intake fields and the farm of Brotherilkeld. This has been in the same family for four generations and is one of the National Trust's biggest farms in the Lakes. Although Brotherilkeld dates from the seventeenth century, there has been a settlement here since Saxon times. In 1242 the monks of Furness Abbey bought the 14,000-acre estate and the land was enclosed towards the end of the thirteenth century. In 1935 the Forestry Commission bought the farm and 7,000 acres of surounding land in Eskdale and the Duddon valley intending to create the 'Hardknott National Forest Park'. While agreement was reached the following year that the heart of Lakeland was to be protected from further encroachment of forestry, it wasn't until 1958 that the head of the two valleys was finally secured with their sale to the National Trust. The National Trust owns eighty hill farms, over 250 cottages and 140,000 acres of the Lake District, nearly a quarter of their total assets and ten times as much as the Furness Abbey monks.

As the valley narrows the river becomes more rocky and, interrupted by little waterfalls, it gradually deepens to still green pools. This is a lovely part of the Esk and a perfect setting for Lingcove Bridge, one of the many stone packhorse bridges which were built in the mid-seventeenth to eighteenth centuries. Above the bridge the route deserts the river to follow Lingcove Beck up towards the still distant Bow Fell beside a narrow ravine of waterfalls and into the hollow of Green Hole beneath Bow Fell.

On the col between Bow Fell and Crinkle Crags is Three Tarns. This is the crossing of the ways where the Low Level Route heads off down The Band for Langdale, while the High Level Route continues along The Crinkles. From Three Tarns to the easy slopes leading down to Red Tarn, the ridge of Crinkle Crags is just a mile in length, a fascinating mile of ins and outs and ups and downs so that not only does it seem much further, but it is often difficult to be sure exactly where you are. And then as evening falls you descend into Langdale, the "Long Valley", beneath a serrated skyline of encircling fells as lengthening shadows chase your footsteps down to the warmth of the farms and the Old Dungeon Ghyll Hotel.

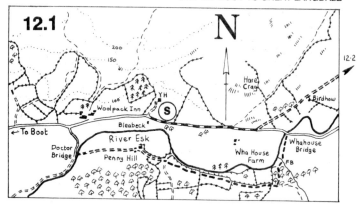

ROUTE DESCRIPTION

JOINT ROUTE

If the night was spent at **Boot** the quickest way to upper Eskdale is to walk up the road past the youth hostel. A less rapid but much prettier alternative is to follow the continuation of the Low Level Route, given on Day 11, to Doctor Bridge where you cross the River Esk and take the track past Penny Hill Farm through the fields. After fording a small stream, turn left down through a wood to the road, then go left over Whahouse Bridge to join the youth hostellers on the track to Taw House.

From **Eskdale Youth Hostel**, walk half a mile up the road and take the track on the left to Taw House. Passing the little cottage of Birdhow, a National Trust holiday property, the fell straight ahead is Hard Knott. On the southern slopes overlooking Eskdale is the Roman Fort of Mediobogdum, whose massive stone walls can just be discerned from here. Taw House was visited by Samuel Taylor Coleridge and the word Taw comes from Towers, the name of the owner at that time. A ladder stile to the left of the farmhouse leads to a path across the field and a footbridge over the River Esk to **Brotherilkeld**, which is spelt Butterilket on old maps and is still pronounced that way.

As you follow the river upstream, there appears at first sight to be nothing remarkable about these fields beside the Esk, but the grassy terraces indicate the successive levels of lakes formed during the Ice Age which created these ancient shorelines. Leaving the enclosing fields the path continues up the river. The rough slopes on the right are Hard Knott and high on the skyline is Eskdale Needle, a tall finger of rock, while on the far side of the river rise the cliffs of Heron Crag.

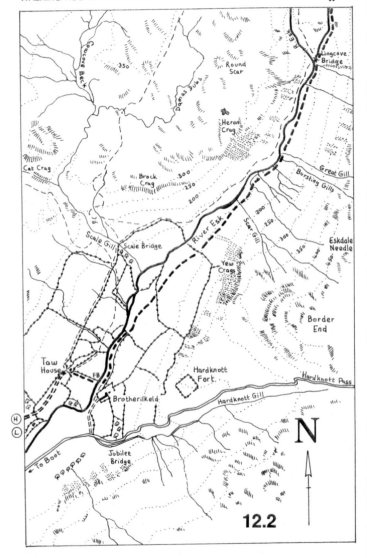

Lingcove Bridge

The river becomes steadily more interesting with a series of little waterfalls and pools and just before Lingcove Bridge is Tongue Pot, two deep, clear green pools linked by a waterfall and overhung by an ash tree. At the bridge the river divides, each tributary with another delectable series of waterfalls.

Like many of the packhorse bridges, **Lingcove Bridge** has been skilfully rebuilt to replace an earlier one which collapsed. The adjacent sheepfold has been in continuous use since medieval times and further up the river at Great Moss are the remains of boundary walls and dykes constructed by the Furness monks around 1284, designed to restrict the sheep but not the deer within the estate.

Don't cross the bridge but follow the path to the right of Lingcove Beck. At last you start to climb purposefully beside a ravine of waterfalls with grand retrospective views of Eskdale. The angle soon eases and the junction with Swinsty Gill is reached. To the left the long ridge of Slight Side climbs to Sca Fell which is separated from Scafell Pike by the great gap of Mickledore. Close at hand is the rocky rise of Pianet Knott, while ahead flanking Ore Gap are Esk Pike and Bow Fell.

After fording Swinsty Gill a slimmer version of the path continues for a further half mile towards Green Hole, the green empty valley below Bow Fell. The little path wanders away from the meandering beck to keep out of the

179

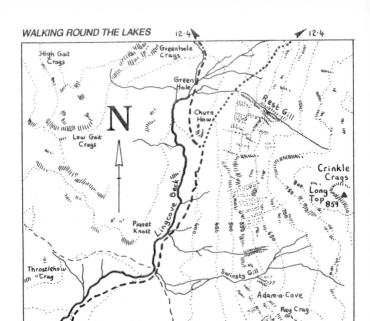

boggy ground and the ways divide before the rocky knoll of **Churn How**.

HIGH LEVEL ROUTE

With little sign of a path, cut across the high ground to the left of Churn How and then follow Yeastyrigg Gill steeply uphill. On the far side of the gill, tucked into the hillside, is a ruined hut, then higher up the path becomes more definite and in just over a mile the red stained earth of **Ore Gap** is reached. This also was part of the Furness monks' estate and in medieval times iron ore from here was taken by packhorse to the smelter at Langstrath in Borrowdale. In the eighteenth century there were plans, which fortunately never materialised, to construct a rack-railway and mine at Ore Gap on a large scale.

The good path along the ridge links Esk Pike and Bow Fell and, after an initially rough start, is easy to follow. By-passing the northern summit of Bow Fell the path climbs to meet the edge at Bowfell Buttress where the ground suddenly falls away and the Langdale Pikes appear on the far side of Mickleden, with Fairfield and the Far Eastern Fells beyond. Continue over the rough boulders following the cairns for a final scramble up to the top of **Bow Fell**, a mass of boulders over and around which you climb to the last

180

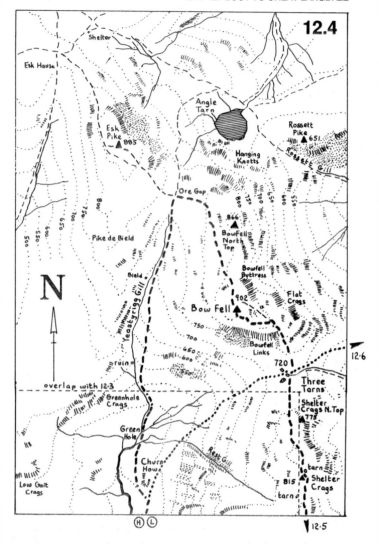

12.4

Shelter

Esk Hause

Angle Tarn

Rossett Pika ▲ 651

Rossett G.

Esk Pike ▲ 885

Hanging Knotts

Ore Gap

800

.866
BowFell North Top

750

Pike de Bield

800

Bield

BowFell Buttress

Flat Crags

650

Bow Fell ▲ 902

750

700

BowFell Links

650

600

ruin

12·6

720

overlap with 12·3

Three Tarns

Greenhole Crags

Shelter Crags N.Top ▲ 775

Green Hole

Rest Gill

Churn Howe

tarn

Low Gait Crags

815

Shelter Crags

tarn

Ⓗ Ⓛ

▼ 12·5

181

Crinkle Crags and Bow Fell from Red Tarn

cairn which marks the summit. Far below to the east the green valley of Langdale runs down to Windermere, in the opposite direction the long valley of Eskdale stretches into the distance and out to the west is the magnificent and now familiar skyline of the Scafells and Great End.

The massive tilted slab of Flat Crags to the east holds the key to the descent. After scrambling down over the boulders by any one of several cairned routes, head east to join the broad path which passes above these enormous slabs before going south down to **Three Tarns**. Although the peaty surface of the col is often churned to a morass and the tarns at first glance not the most attractive, they are a superb foreground, which often reflects the distant Scafells.

If time is short or the weather miserable the Low Level Route can be joined at Three Tarns. The path down The Band goes off from the lowest point on the col and the fields of Langdale will be reached in under an hour.

Ahead is the delightful switchback ridge of Crinkle Crags. Passing Three Tarns the High Level Route continues along the ridge following a clear path which winds its way over and around the many minor tops. After passing the rocky outcrop of Shelter Crags North Top, the path climbs to reach a small tarn between rocky knolls of which the far one, topped with a small cairn, is the summit of **Shelter Crags**.

The path continues, dipping to another small tarn and then climbing past

182

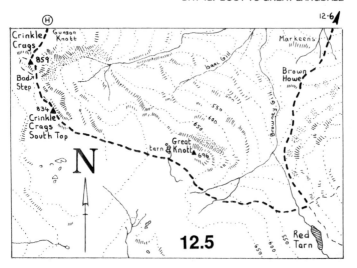

Gunson Knott, the first of the Crinkles. Two more Crinkles are passed and the gully of Mickle Door before climbing to Long Top, the highest of the Crinkles and the summit of **Crinkle Crags**. The northernmost cairn marks the highest point from which all the major summits of the Lake District are in view. The Scafells continue to dominate the west while far away in the north Skiddaw and Blencathra can be seen on the distant skyline. This is the least spectacular view of the Langdale Pikes, diminished and flattened when seen from above, but eastwards are the Helvellyn and Fairfield ranges with the High Street fells beyond and in the far distance, the blue shape between Pike o' Blisco and Wetherlam is the flat top of Ingleborough, some 37 miles away.

The main path to the left of the summit negotiates the Bad Step, an awkward drop by a wedged chockstone. This can easily be avoided by the less nimble by walking a short way north-west along Long Top and then taking the easy path to the left which avoids all such obstacles.

The path now continues in a straightforward manner over the last Crinkle, before descending the gentle grassy slopes between Great Knott and Cold Pike. As it curves round the head of Browney Gill and down to **Red Tarn**, the aerial view of the ground at the col reveals grass-covered mounds, the remains of old iron workings dating from 1860.

Ahead lies Pike o' Blisco, but after a long day this is better saved for tomorrow, so crossing the stream take the red path north down into the valley. After an initially steep descent over red stained earth and rocks the

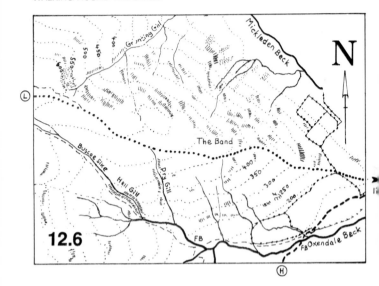

angle eases above the cleft of Browney Gill where a backward glance reveals the waterfalls tumbling down from beneath Great Knott. After passing Brown Howe the path, which has been recently repaired by the National Trust, makes easy work of the descent. As you go down, the Langdale Pikes grow in stature until, crossing Oxendale Beck at the memorial footbridge to follow the track up to Stool End farm, the Pikes once more resume their rightful dominance of Langdale. It is then only half a mile down the tarmac lane to the Old Dungeon Ghyll Hotel at the head of **Great Langdale**.

LOW LEVEL ROUTE

Diverging from the beck the route stays on the path to pass to the right of **Churn How**, climbing across the rough lower slopes of Long Top and the tumbled boulders of Rest Gill. The path, now cairned and more obvious, rises towards the col with to the left the rock buttresses, screes and deep furrows of Bowfell Links. Looking back on reaching **Three Tarns**, clear weather may reveal Sca Fell and Scafell Pike reflected in their still waters.

Passing between two of the tarns to the far side of the col, the High Level Route can be joined by turning right on the main path towards the Crinkles.

Heading for Langdale the wide stony path leads down **The Band**, meaning "The Boundary". To the left the Langdale Pikes gradually increase in stature

184

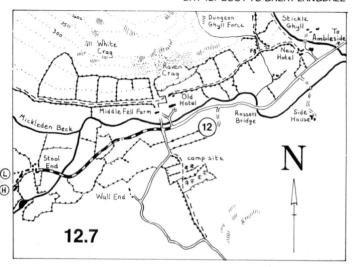

12.7

before disappearing as the path passes to the right of the ridge, and to the south Red Tarn gleams above the red stripe of the path between Pike o'Blisco and Crinkle Crags. Lower down the Langdale Pikes reappear, having grown during their absence and now towering above the flat green fields of Langdale. The long ridge which divides the two valleys of Oxendale and Mickleden terminates abruptly at Stool End farm and it is then only half a mile down the tarmac lane to the Old Dungeon Ghyll Hotel at the head of **Great Langale**.

GREAT LANGDALE

From the little village of Chapel Stile to the head of Great Langdale, a narrow road winds its way up the valley bounded on either side by unyielding solid stone walls. At the foot of the fells, small intake fields cluster round the sheep farms and in the spring the valley is loud with the cry of newborn lambs. This is one of Lakeland's loveliest valleys where no "development", no "improvement", is allowed to destroy its beauty as most of the valley is owned by the National Trust. It was the historian George Trevelyn who in 1928 bought Stool End and Wall End farms and also the Old Dungeon Ghyll Hotel and donated them to the Trust and this was later followed by the gift of more buildings.

On either side of Great Langdale and especially at its head, steep crags

185

Stool End Farm

of rough rock line the fellside. The valley owes its rugged shape to the action of glaciers which formed high on the fells and flowed down to Windermere. The flat section above Church Stile was once the bed of a shallow lake and after heavy rain can still become one again despite much flood prevention work. Below the memorial footbridge over Oxendale Beck is a series of weirs and a reservoir which will hopefully prevent a recurrence of the flood which in August 1966 swept away walls, bridges and even some of the road.

At the head of the valley Ward Lock's Red Guide of the 1950s warns: *after this there is no practicable motoring road to Blea Tarn and Little Langdale* and although it has since been metalled the comment is still true when at weekends cars jam the narrow pass with its hairpin bends.

At the foot of the pass are a campsite and two hotels. The campsite, for tents only, is well screened with trees and is very popular throughout the year. Looking down from snow-clad hills we've been surprised to see it almost full in mid-winter. The Old Dungeon Ghyll Hotel, known affectionately as the ODG, holds many happy memories of family holidays when our children were small and Sid Cross was the landlord. Sid was also the leader of the Langdale Mountain Rescue Team and his wife Jamie was the first lady to lead Central Buttress on Sca Fell, at the time the hardest rock climb in the

186

country. The rival New Dungeon Ghyll, a little further down the valley, after a spell as an outdoor pursuits centre, is once again a hotel. The adjacent building was converted in 1986 to the Stickle Barn, a pub offering food and bunkhouse accommodation.

Originally statesmen-farms, the two hotels are here because of the Victorian passion for waterfalls. The Dungeon Ghyll Force, which still retains the picturesque Victorian spelling of ghyll for gill, was much admired, visited and written about. Wordsworth couldn't resist a poem about *that black and dreadful rent* and his friend Coleridge featured *that deep romantic chasm* in *Kubla Khan:*

> *And from this chasm, with ceaseless turmoil seething,*
> *As if this earth in thick fast pants were breathing,*
> *A mighty fountain momently was forced;*

But waterfalls are less popular these days; it is the mountain summits that are the attraction and most of today's walkers hurry past on their way to visit the Langdale Pikes.

Pike o'Blisco from Great Langdale

187

The Coniston fells from Torver

| HIGH LEVEL ROUTE | Distance 8½ miles | Ascent 4,000ft |
| LOW LEVEL ROUTE | Distance 7 miles | Ascent 1,600ft |

ROUTE SUMMARY

High Level Route A strenuous aperitif of the rocky Pike o'Blisco is followed by a descent to the Three Shire Stone, at the top of Wrynose Pass, where a good path climbs the grassy slopes of Wetside Edge onto the Coniston fells. Having reached Great Carrs, it is then an easy walk over Swirl How and Brim Fell to Coniston Old Man before descending to the Coppermines Valley.

Low Level Route This is not just for bad weather and offers strong competition, passing Blea Tarn in the combe between Great and Little Langdale. Continuing across the lower slopes of Wetherlam and up beside the ravine of Tilberthwaite Gill, Hole Rake is crossed to reach the Coppermines Valley.

Facing the Old Dungeon Ghyll Hotel across the head of Great Langdale, Pike o'Blisco is an ascent few can resist with its steep and challenging slopes rising nearly two thousand feet from Oxendale. Above the rough rocks, crags and boulders which reach down to the flat green fields of Langdale, the summit stands against the sky and the ascent via Redacre Gill is one of the best.

Reaching the summit you look back, down the long valley of Langdale to Windermere in the distance and then across at the mountains. The Langdale Pikes and many of the distant fells are in view, but the most impressive are Bow Fell and Crinkle Crags whose black-shadowed great buttresses rising above the lower slopes ring the head of the valley.

The circuit of the fell, however, also holds enjoyment as at the foot of the eastern slopes lies Blea Tarn, from whose southern shore is one of the finest views in the Lakes. On a calm, clear day the Langdale Pikes are seen reflected in its surface and set exactly in the right place, a rocky headland bearing a clump of pine trees juts into the lake.

Beside the lake is an isolated farm, the home of the Solitary in Wordsworth's long poem *The Excursion*:

> *A quiet treeless nook, with two green fields,*
> *A liquid pool that glittered in the sun,*
> *And one bare dwelling; one abode, no more!*

Wordsworth also quoted this description of Bleatarn House in his *Guide*

Fell Foot, Little Langdale

to the Lakes, but with an addendum *no longer strictly applicable, on account of recent plantation.* Although the rhododendrons and larch are later additions, some of the trees were planted by Bishop Llandaff in the eighteenth century.

Because it was so steep that only a strong horse could cross it, the road that has its foot in Little Langdale and its head at the Three Shire Stone was called Wrynose Pass, the pass of the stallion. From here it is then over or around the mountains. It is possible to romp across the Coniston fells in a day: Wetherlam, Swirl How, Grey Friar, Dow Crag, Coniston Old Man, the lot. It isn't even terribly strenuous, the paths are good and there's no stumbling over rocks and stones as on the Scafells, but like most of the Lakeland hills the Coniston fells are best enjoyed in a leisurely fashion.

We reached Coniston Old Man slowly, one already heavy rucksack topped with a full water container, for the night was to be spent beside the huge pile of stone, the "Old Man" of the mountain's title. It was early evening and the crowds that throng the summit at midday had long since gone. The air hardly stirred. A midge borne aloft by the warm air found its evening meal putting up the tent on a grassy expanse beside the cairn. Coniston Water shimmered in the distance and the hills became blue silhouettes as the sun slowly sank towards the horizon. Dinner was followed by coffee and we were joined by a young couple with a dog. It was her first mountain and neither seemed surprised to find us camped on the summit. Gradually the air chilled, the sky turned from blue to azure and then to black. One by one the stars came out and we lay in our sleeping bags watching the universe.

The descent to the Coppermines Valley comes as a shock for the first time. Who allowed this to happen? Unlike the mellowed mysterious depths of the slate quarries, here is exploitation in the raw. Nature has tried to heal the scars, but it will perhaps be centuries before the sterile screes of the copper mines are clothed again.

No-one is quite sure what to do about the Coppermines Valley. It's already spoilt say some, why not a store for deadly chlorine here? And they have, too, a sinister enclave above the hostel - "Check the leak detector before entering." Another quarry, what a good idea! - "Beware of blasting." Yet after the first shock the valley is seen to be not wholly spoilt. The youth hostel and the adjacent climbing hut stand on the scree tips of the mines, while industrial archaeologists rescue and restore a few remaining buildings, leats and levels to show what once was here when nearly a thousand men toiled in these hills. Somehow the valley retains its spirit and violets bloom beneath the cliffs and if Low Water is perhaps an unnatural blue prompted by copper rather than reflected sky, there is still the magnificent waterfall into Boulder valley and countless corners unspoilt by man.

Copper has probably been mined in the valley of Red Dell Beck since Roman times. In the late sixteenth century the Elizabethan Company of Mines Royal was founded and expert German miners were brought here from Keswick to work the mines. The copper ore was at first transported by packhorse to the Keswick smelters, then at the end of the eighteenth century it was shipped down the lake and taken by carts to the quay at Greenodd on the Duddon Estuary. The mines were at their most prosperous in the middle of the nineteenth century with as many as thirteen water-wheels used to power the crushing, refining and smelting mills. After this production gradually declined and copper mining ceased around 1915.

When copper mining became uneconomical the local slate was quarried instead. This is a tough rock and as it can be easily polished it is used to face buildings. Recently the small quarry on the far side of the beck was reopened and was working in 1990, but now the rest of the industry has gone.

We came down from the Coniston fells one October afternoon to a friendly welcome at a farm overlooking the town. It was a good meal and our fellow guests were a group of men enthusiastically anticipating a long weekend on the private miniature railway which we had never suspected lay hidden in the trees nearby. Mother, aged over eighty who was staying while she recovered from a fall, had recently baked thirty christmas cakes for friends and relatives. After dinner there was coffee by the fireside and a long chat with our host. This lady, who admitted she had just reached sixty, not only looked after the visitors but also, single-handed, managed the farm whose sheep roam the slopes of Coniston Old Man. "How many dogs do you have?" we asked, marvelling at her energy. "None," she replied, "I use my motor bike."

ROUTE DESCRIPTION

HIGH LEVEL ROUTE

From the **Old Dungeon Ghyll Hotel** turn right on the road and follow it round the corner. After passing Wall End farm and the dry stone barn which dates from late medieval times, the road zigzags up the hill. In the 1966 flood huge boulders were tumbled down the beck and the road was washed away creating a scene of devastation. At the second hairpin bend a good path sets off above Redacre Gill climbing gradually to ford two becks. Becoming much more rough and eroded the path then climbs steeply before levelling out on Wrynose Fell. The summit of **Pike o'Blisco** is now only a little further and after negotiating a couple of rocky staircases, the twin tops are reached. The northernmost rocky knoll, which is the highest, looks down on Langdale far below. Across the valley are the Langdale Pikes with Skiddaw and Helvellyn on either side in the distance. Bow Fell dominates the head of the valley while to the south the horseshoe of the Coniston fells beckons.

A good but rough path descends south-west towards **Red Tarn** from which yesterday's high route went down into Great Langdale. On reaching the red-stained path turn left to pass above the tarn and then descend gently to the left of the infant River Duddon for about a mile to reach the **Three Shire Stone** which is just below the summit of Wrynose Pass. This stone pillar, which marked the junction of the counties of Cumberland, Westmorland and Lancashire, has one face inscribed 'Lancashire WF 1816', the date the stone was erected, but it became obsolete in 1974 with the formation of the new county of Cumbria.

From the summit of the pass a little path heads south up Wet Side Edge. Below, the River Duddon snakes down Wrynose Bottom towards the cone of Harter Fell and Hardknott Pass. Half-way up the path appears to change its mind and have second thoughts, but stay with it for soon there is another steep bit and a hairpin bend and the edge is reached with little effort. Ahead

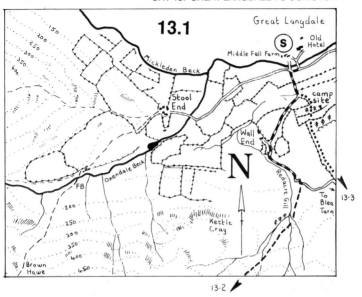

13·2

across the combe is Wetherlam, tomorrow's objective, its north face falling steeply to Greenburn Beck. The grassy ridge rises gradually to Little Carrs and then the path forks. Staying by the edge, climb through tumbled stones to **Great Carrs** where a cairn on an outcrop marks the highest point. Westwards across a grassy col is Grey Friar with the isolated Harter Fell beyond, while ahead lies Swirl How and the long ridge of Brim Fell leading to Coniston Old Man and the sharply pointed Dow Crag.

It is an easy stroll over stones and grass round the edge to **Swirl How**, passing a cross which was erected by a party of air cadets in 1982 beside the sad wreckage of a Halifax bomber. The aircraft crashed on October 22, 1944 while on a training flight and far below on Broad Slack more pieces lie scattered on the screes.

From the pointed cairn the broad ridge runs south gradually narrowing to Levers Hause in three-quarters of a mile. A short cut may be made here by following the path left down to Levers Water and the Coppermines Valley. Originally enlarged for the mines, Levers Water is now used as a reservoir and beyond it Coniston village and Coniston Water are now in view. To the right is Seathwaite Tarn, which has been enlarged to form a reservoir for Barrow. While few flowers grow on the acid moorland around the tarn and it might be assumed that it was always so, it is the rain of 10,000 years which

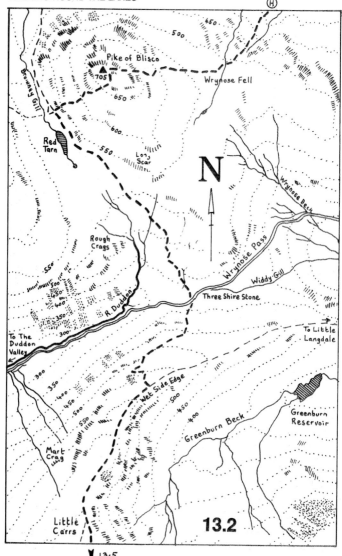

has washed all the goodness from the soil for just after the Ice Age the freshly broken rock sustained many more plants including the now rare Jacob's Ladder. From Levers Hause it is an easy stroll to reach **Brim Fell** with a broad stony path leading to the grand cairn, the only point of interest on this flat, mainly grassy summit.

Coniston Old Man looks only a hop, skip and jump away along the ridge. Below to the left is Low Water and to the right Dow Crag rises in splendid cliffs from the screes above the hidden Goats Water. **The Old Man of Coniston**, to give him his correct title, has a huge cairn mounted on a stone plinth which is visible for miles, dwarfing the adjacent and lower OS trig point. This is almost the edge of the Lake District. Morecambe Bay glistens to the south and eastwards are Coniston Water and Windermere, but the eye of the true fellwalker turns northwards towards the hills.

The Three Shire Stone

The descent to Coniston follows the tourist route, a broad path zigzagging steeply and stonily through the remains of old slate quarries to the startlingly blue **Low Water**. Heading towards Coniston Water the path, in many places with the original paving, continues down through the quarries with much of interest in the way of old levels, buildings and machinery. Piles of slate waste rise on either hand, railway lines tip over the edge and at one point the way is crossed by two massive cables of an aerial ropeway which hang in a great curve from ruined towers. The path becomes a track and at the first junction you can see the whitewashed building of the youth hostel straight ahead on the far side of the Coppermines Valley.

If your destination is **Coniston** or Holly How Youth Hostel, stay on the main path forking left at the next junction to Miners Bridge, then follow the Low Level Route for Day 14.

If you are staying at the **Coppermines Youth Hostel,** the beck, a large boggy area and the re-opened Brandy Crag Quarry intervene. To avoid these turn left along the old mine road. At the road end, past the spoil heaps and an old level, descend to cross Levers Water Beck at a new bridge, erected on August 11, 1982 and the youth hostel is now only a short stroll down the track.

LOW LEVEL ROUTE

From the **Old Dungeon Ghyll Hotel** turn right and then go round the corner and up the road to a stile into the campsite. A footpath beside the wall leads round to the right through an area that is usually full of small tents to a kissing gate in the trees and uphill across a field to a small wood. Continue climbing beside the wall. To the right Bow Fell guards the head of Great Langdale standing between the twin valleys of Mickleden and Oxendale where the white water of Whorneyside Force plunges down, while on looking back across Langdale, the Langdale Pikes rise dramatically. The road is rejoined at the top of the pass where there is a memorial seat with a double dedication.

Cross the road and follow the path down to **Blea Tarn**, the setting of a large portion of Wordsworth's epic poem *The Excursion*. Across the fields, below the slopes of Lingmoor Fell, is the whitewashed Bleatarn House. An isolated monkey puzzle tree stands incongruously aloof, then a kissing gate designed to accommodate generously proportioned visitors leads into mixed woodland where the surroundings of the tarn have the feel of the garden of a stately home. At the end of the tarn a short detour left may be rewarded by the classic view of the Langdale Pikes mirrored in the water. Take the newly crazy-paved way to the right of the outflow from the tarn through a kissing gate onto the open fellside.

The path keeps high above Bleamoss Beck dashing through its little rocky gorge, then bends right above a wall and round Blea Moss, a wide boggy valley. Below to the left above a ruin is a large cast iron table propped on end which was evidently used for target practice and the unfenced road is soon joined at the foot of Wrynose Pass. Unsurfaced before 1939, the road was so badly damaged by army vehicles training during the war that it was resurfaced using concrete for much of the way.

Turn left towards Little Langdale along a wide grassy verge until the road narrows to pass **Fell Foot**. Once an inn, this has the Fletchers Fleming Arms high above the door and hidden behind the farm is a terraced Thing Mound where it is thought the Vikings met in council. Passing the buildings the road bends and then a few yards further on turn right over Fell Foot Bridge across the infant River Brathay. The river, which marked the boundary between Westmorland and Lancashire, rises on Wrynose Pass near the Three Shire Stone. It has an eventful short life flowing through Little Langdale Tarn and Elterwater and over two waterfalls, Colwith Force and Skelghyll Force, before arriving sedately at Windermere.

The walled track crosses the fields to **Bridge End**, beside Greenburn

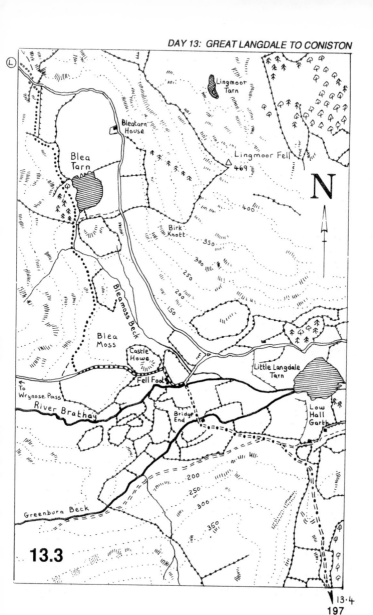

Lingmoor Tarn

Bleatarn House

Blea Tarn

Lingmoor Fell
△ 469

Birk Knott

400

350

300

250

200

150

N

Bleamoss Beck

Blea Moss

Castle Howe

Fell Foot

Little Langdale Tarn

To Wrynose Pass

River Brathay

Bridge End

Low Hall Garth

200

250

300

350

Greenburn Beck

13.3

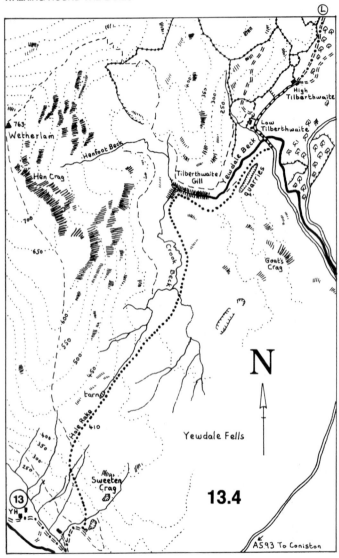

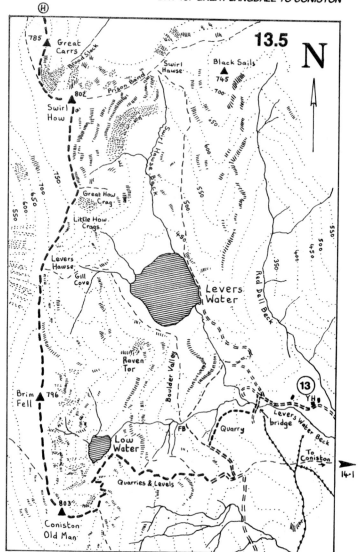

Beck, then climbs bending left. Above Little Langdale Tarn ignore the track leading down to Low Hall Garth and fork right up a rougher track. After passing disused quarries on the hillside to the right and others hidden in trees to the left, the old road descends gently to **High Tilberthwaite**. Going through the farmyard the lane is followed to Low Tilberthwaite where the end house has a spinning gallery.

After crossing the bridge over Yewdale Beck, climb the path which zigzags up by the slate tips. Enticing pathways into the huge quarry, which dates from the eighteenth century, provide grandstand views of the rock climbers. The path gradually rises to the left of **Tilberthwaite Gill** in its steep-sided ravine. The gill was a popular excursion with the Victorians and it was once criss-crossed with bridges. A path diverges to cross the stream at a new bridge, but keeping to the higher path a rocky stairway climbs above the gorge which in spring is bright with primroses. At the head of the ravine swing left keeping above Crook Beck. The indistinct, but cairned path crosses the moor-like fellside to join an old mine track which climbs past disused quarries and the black hole of a copper mine and soon Coniston Old Man appears ahead with its summit cairn outlined against the sky. Passing a reedy tarn nearly on the col, the path rounds a corner above **Hole Rake** for a birds-eye view of the Coppermines Valley. It is now downhill all the way as the path slants down with Coniston Water in the distance, to more disused quarries and then zigzags to join the road.

Walkers bound for **Coniston** should turn left and refer to tomorrow's Low Level Route for directions, but for those with a bed booked at **Coniston Coppermines Youth Hostel**, journey's end is only a few yards to the right up the track.

CONISTON

The grey mining village of Coniston, set back from the lakeside on the flats of slate and shale of the Silurian rocks beside Coniston Water has not entirely succumbed to the tourist trade. It has some real shops and real people live and work here. On the far side of the 5½-mile long lake the hills are rounded and wooded, but above the village tower the craggy Borrowdale Volcanics. It is this junction in the geology which resulted in the minerals which brought mining to Coniston in the eighteenth century. Last century there were several hundreds of mines and to serve these the railway opened in 1859. It was linked to the Furness Railway near Broughton till 1958 when the line was closed. In addition to the Coppermines Youth Hostel, there is a second and grander one which is passed at the begining of Day 14 on the Low Route. This was a former guest house and stands in its own landscaped grounds.

The Coppermines Youth Hostel, surrounded by the remains of a once thriving nineteenth century copper industry, stands on the main ore processing area. Here the ore was sorted, before being crushed, a labour-intensive activity carried out by women and children as well as the men. The finely ground ore was then separated from the waste by a process known as buddling, in which water floated off the surplus rock, leaving the heavier ore. The chief problem of the mines, some of which were more than a thousand feet below the surface, was water, which had to be pumped from the shafts. However, while water in a mine is a problem, water on the surface was a valuable asset providing a cheap and plentiful power supply. Great water-wheels were built to provide power for the pumps and also to drive the ore-separating machinery. The Great Wheel of 1830, 30 feet in diameter and 7 feet across, was replaced by one even larger at 44 feet diameter and 9 feet wide in 1852, but there were several other wheels all fed by mill-races from Red Dell Beck. Copper mines are often vertical fissures and the levels which enter the workings are not really tunnels, their floors are merely rubble and clay supported by rotting timbers over an abyss. More than any other mines these are potentially lethal to enter.

On the far shore of the lake and facing The Old Man is Brantwood, the home of John Ruskin from 1872 until his death in 1900. Ruskin, who was the first Slade Professor of Fine Art at Oxford and who gave his name to Ruskin College, was so fond of the Lake District that when he heard this house with its view of Coniston Old Man was for sale, he wrote *any place opposite Coniston Old Man must be beautiful* and bought it immediately without even coming to see it. He renovated the derelict property and added a turret which overlooked the lake. Brantwood, which is now open to the public, also houses a Wainwright exhibition which has the original manuscripts of the Coniston Old Man chapter of *The Southern Fells*. In true museum tradition there is also the great man's jacket, pipe and glasses, a pen and a bottle of ink, but these dead mementos contrast strangely with the living drawings which recreate his beloved fells.

Another devotee of Coniston was Donald Campbell, but the appeal for him was in the long, straight lake. This was ideal for his boat Bluebird with which he set the world speed record in 1959 reaching a speed of 276.33mph. Attempting the record again in 1967 he was killed when his boat somersaulted at over 300mph. The friendships formed in those hectic days of his attempts on the world speed record are still maintained with members of the team coming together every year for a reunion dinner at Coniston.

Just off the main street there is an old-fashioned museum, the Ruskin Museum which has an odd assortment of Ruskin memorabilia, some geological and archaeological specimens and some photos of Donald Campbell and his boat. There is a National Park information centre and boats can be hired on the lake which was once known as Thurston's Mere. Since 1980 there has also been the Victorian steam yacht, the *Gondola*. Built in 1859 it was acquired by the National Trust in 1976, restored and put back into service.

Coniston honours its sons with a large slate cross from the Tilberthwaite quarries marking Ruskin's grave in the little churchyard which he chose for his last resting place rather than a tomb in Westminster Abbey, while a slate seat on the green stands in memory of Donald Campbell, whose grave is Coniston Water.

The Coppermines Youth Hostel

Low Tilberthwaite

| HIGH LEVEL ROUTE | Distance 9 miles | Ascent 2,050ft |
| LOW LEVEL ROUTE | Distance 9 miles | Ascent 850ft |

ROUTE SUMMARY

High Level Route Those intent on the hills need only pray for a fine morning as, although Wetherlam tops 2,500 feet, a mere 130 feet lower than Coniston Old Man, it will be attained before lunch. Thereafter all is downhill and the afternoon may be spent visiting Colwith Force, set amid the bluebell woods, before joining the Low Route for tea at Skelwith Bridge and a leisurely stroll past Elterwater to finish.

Low Level Route Turning away from the hills, you walk over the fields and through the woods to the famous beauty spot of Tarn Hows set amid pine trees between Coniston Water and the head of Windermere. Continuing through attractive woodland the two routes join before Skelwith Bridge.

Separated from the rest of the Coniston fells by the gap of Swirl Hawse, Wetherlam only attracts a small fraction of the numbers that toil up Coniston Old Man every year. But while the Old Man looks down on the quarries and spoil of the copper mines, with steel cables and toppled pylons all on open view, Wetherlam's legacy of its industrial past is more often underground and hidden from sight. The history is still there, though, and the mountain's sides are pierced by innumerable holes, levels and shafts leading to an underground lost empire.

Also hidden, at least from the Coniston side, is Wetherlam Edge, one of the mountain's most attractive features, a rocky rib descending towards Little Langdale. This north-eastern side of Wetherlam, where trees clothe huge piles of discarded rock from the abandoned quarries, is described by Wainwright as *scenically one of the loveliest in Lakeland* and it is especially delightful to descend from the wild rocky tops to these woods where in spring celandines, bluebells and red campion contrast with the white flowers of wood anemones and wood sorrel.

Our usual approach to the Coniston fells is up the broad south ridge of Wetherlam from the Coppermines Valley and with the rest of the Coniston fells still to be tackled there is little time to linger. Explorations for this book, however, brought us to the mountain late one evening and we pitched camp amid the wild violets scattered on these southern slopes. From the doorway of our tent we looked across at Coniston Old Man, while far below, stretching away towards Ulverston, was the blue of Coniston Water.

Wetherlam from above Blea Tarn

It was on these southern slopes too that ascending one cold, clear December morning we saw high above the tops a flock of geese strung out in a long line and as we watched, it divided and reformed, each bird choreographed in a silent stately dance. Our destination that day was Great Langdale at the start of a three-day weekend in the Lakes and our rucksacks were light as we were staying in style at the Old Dungeon Ghyll Hotel. Weekends like this in midwinter create more memories in three days than do three weeks in a city office.

If, however, the clouds are down and Wetherlam must be left for another day, then the Low Level Route is by no means second best for this way leads to Tarn Hows. Considering that over 750,000 people come here every year, it's a miracle it hasn't been trampled to death and the tarn filled with the debris of a million picnics. But it looks lovely still, the perfect picture postcard scene, and even if it has to be carefully tidied up after every bank holiday, the National Trust certainly does a good job. Although it has all the charm of unspoilt nature, Tarn Hows is in fact man-made. Constructed from two or three adjoining tarns, the surroundings were landscaped by the Marshalls of Monk Coniston in the late eighteenth century. The tarn, which was once prosaically dammed to provide water power for a mill, now grows water lilies. Still known as Marshall's Tarn by local people, Tarn Hows is named after the farm of the same name. In 1929 Beatrix Potter bought the Monk Coniston estate, promptly selling half of it, including Tarn Hows, to the National Trust, the money for the purchase being a gift from Sir S.H.Scott, a local man. From the slopes above the tarn Coniston Water is in view, the Langdale Pikes appear to the north-west above the trees, and to the north-east is Helvellyn.

Little Langdale has been left as a hanging valley by the last glacier to flow down Great Langdale and where the River Brathay drops from Little to Great Langdale is the waterfall of Colwith Force. This was at one time a great tourist attraction and with a series of cascades and falls totalling ninety feet in height, it is certainly one of the more spectacular waterfalls in the Lakes, but it is neglected nowadays. Skelwith Force just above the slate works at Skelwith Bridge seems to be preferred and the twenty-foot fall, which carries the greatest volume of water of all Lakeland waterfalls, is seldom without a group of admirers teetering on the edge. The waterfall here is over a ridge of hard rock which resisted the scouring of the Great Langdale glaciers.

The tea at Skelwith Bridge is something we look forward to. On one occasion, electing to sit outside, we carried the tray into the garden followed very attentively, their eyes watching every move, by four dogs and three cats. We are becoming connoisseurs of Lakeland teas. It all started many years ago with the magnificent spreads provided by Sid Cross at the ODG which tempted us back far too early off the hills, but afternoon teas are getting harder to find these days. At one time it seemed every cottage had its little sign, a few tables set out with a clean cloth and a supply of fresh scones and rum butter, but now everything, even the jam, seems to be wrapped in plastic. We had almost given up on teas until last summer and a torrentially wet week backpacking round the Lakes. We were camping wild every night up on the fells, which meant that at teatime invariably we were passing through a village or town. Tea provided a temporary refuge from the rain and we sampled everything from snack bar to grand hotel. We finished the week still wet, but several pounds heavier!

ROUTE DESCRIPTION

HIGH LEVEL ROUTE

From **Coniston Coppermines Youth Hostel** walk down the valley for a short way and then cross the footbridge to pass in front of the row of miners' cottages. Just beyond take the track which climbs up the hill and bends right to an old quarry where you turn off left on a minor path to slant up the hillside to **Hole Rake**.

Just before the highest point of Hole Rake is reached, a small cairned path goes off to the left to wander up through the rocks following the southern ridge of Wetherlam, where in the spring violets and wood sorrel can be found. As you climb, the main Coniston ridge appears ahead with Black Sails, the far end of the Wetherlam summit ridge, visible to the right of Swirl How, but the huge bulk of Lower Hows obscures the summit of Wetherlam itself. Below

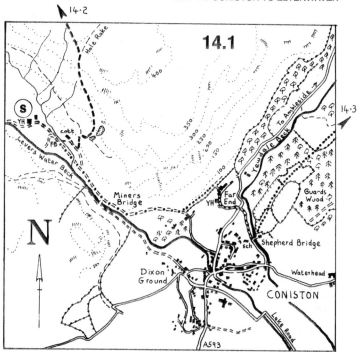

to the right is the flattish top of Yewdale Fells with its long abandoned quarries
and mine levels and beyond is the head of Coniston Water. The path turns
away before a cairn on the final knoll of the ridge is reached and makes its
way easily over grass. Although the lower slopes are quite boggy there are
few if any streams, but to the right is one of Wetherlam's surprises, two little
tarns, seldom visited as they are by-passed by the main path. The first top
reached has a nice cairn and an excellent view of Tilberthwaite far below, but
it is not the summit though it can easily be mistaken in mist for the true one.
Wetherlam summit is 250 yards beyond across a slight dip and with a large
jumbled cairn. Nearly the whole of yesterday's High Level Route over the
Coniston fells can now be seen and the previous day's too, over Crinkle
Crags and Bow Fell. Beyond is the day before that, Sca Fell and Scafell Pike,
while to the north, the unique and easily recognised skyline of the Langdale
Pikes is for tomorrow, the final day.

Falling away steeply directly from the summit, **Wetherlam Edge**, the north-

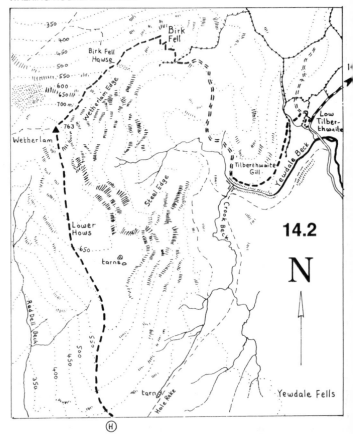

east ridge, has a clear cairned path making an interesting if slightly awkward descent. There are many variations with a choice of little paths and scrambles over white rocks which look as if they have been bleached by the sun. In the Greenburn valley to the left, is a now disused reservoir which produced a head of water for the mine workings downstream. At the bottom a narrow ridge leads to Birk Fell, but before the final knoll is reached turn off right down a zigzag path. Though the path is safe enough, on either hand is evidence of old copper mines with many narrow, hand-worked levels, and while all old workings are hazardous to enter, copper mines are particularly so, with rotting timber floors over deep and dangerous shafts. Scattered groups of larch trees relieve the bleakness of the fell, but the many tree stumps testify that the whole of this area was wooded until the early nineteenth century, the timber being used by the miners for pit props and for charcoal.

The path joins an old mine road and for the rest of the day the going is easy underfoot. Passing the old levels and spoil heaps of the Tilberthwaite Mine, which started in Elizabethan times and closed in 1942, the track then passes high above the ravine of **Tilberthwaite Gill**. The drop beside the path is precipitous and it must have been a hazardous occupation coming along here with a loaded cart. On the far bank the National Trust has planted trees to help the woodland regenerate, no natural seedlings being safe from the voracious sheep. Veering away from the gill the track passes a fenced-off zinc mine where you can clearly see the dangers of exploring old workings, the apparently solid floor of the tunnel being composed of earth heaped upon rotten timbers over an earlier shaft. Crossing a stile and stream the path emerges onto the High Fell Quarry road where you turn right down to Low Tilberthwaite with its picturesque spinning gallery.

Turning left along the lane it is an easy quarter of a mile to **High Tilberthwaite** where after passing through the farmyard you take the lower path which goes right to Little Langdale. The unsurfaced track leads through bluebell woods and by old slate spoil heaps where quarrying began around the middle of the eighteenth century. Keeping to the main track fork right in half a mile just before the second gate and go downhill to a T-junction where you turn left. There is more pleasant walking through Moss Rigg Wood by huge, disused quarry tips, fast disappearing beneath the canopy of trees. Then after passing an unexpected modern house, the River Brathay is reached at a ford and footbridge which lead to Little Langdale. A detour of a few yards to the left along the unsurfaced road leads to a track up into the quarries where a short level enters the enormous Cathedral Cave. This massive man-made cavern was created when the slate was mined rather than quarried away and it has a huge supporting pillar with a 'window' high above.

Don't cross the river, but turn back sharply leaving the wood on the now tarmacked track and climb briefly to Stang End. Rounding the cottage the unfenced road leads to High Park, in medieval times a sheep farm owned by the monks of Furness Abbey, and here you turn left through the farm buildings to follow a bridleway across the fields to the wood.

Immediately on entering the wood take the permissive path downhill to **Colwith Force**, a delightful spot which in spring is carpeted with wood sorrel and bluebells. The river is overhung by trees and the falls are best seen from below where twin spouts drop into the gloomy depths of a deep pool. Keep beside the river until a stile is reached at the road where a short cut can be

Tarn Hows

made to Elterwater just over a mile away. Turn right and in a few yards left over another stile signed 'Skelwith Bridge' to join the Low Route across the fields.

LOW LEVEL ROUTE

Take the track down the valley from **Coniston Coppermines Youth Hostel** past Miners Bridge until the intake wall on the left is reached just before the road becomes metalled. Coniston village with its hotels and bed and breakfast houses is straight on down the lane, but the route turns left over a stile following the wall for 250 yards to a gate. A walled path leads down to the cottages at Far End where you turn right passing the stately mansion of **Holly How Youth Hostel**, and out to the main road.

Go straight across and down the lane, then opposite the smart new primary school cross Shepherd Bridge and double back beside Yewdale Beck into the fields. Beyond the large oak trees is a mock castle supposedly built by the Marshalls of Monk Coniston as an ornate kennel for their dogs. Go through a kissing gate on its left then up the fields where, from a gorse-bedecked bank, there are grand views of Coniston Water, the village and the

210

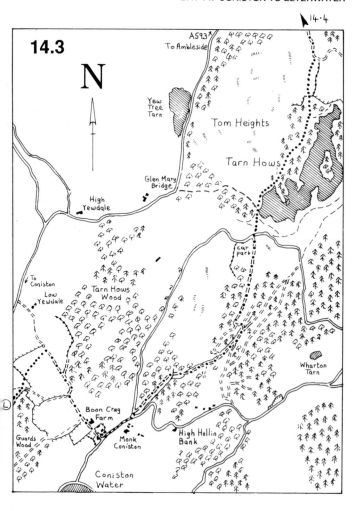

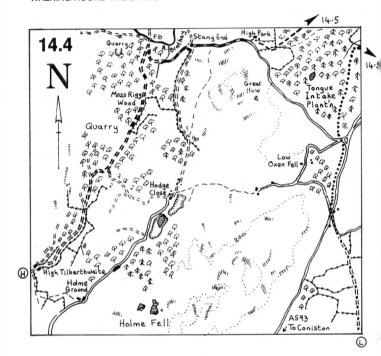

Old Man. At the top of the field a fenced enclosure protects livestock from a row of fine old yew trees. The wood is entered at a stile and then emerging into the open the path continues in the same direction across a field to a gate and through a second field to reach an old road at a stile. Many of the trees in this area were blown over by a freak wind in February 1990 which corkscrewed through, uprooting and snapping ancient beeches, oaks and pines in a few seconds, leaving a narrow trail of devastation behind. Turning right on the track the banks are covered in spring with violets and primroses, stitchwort, wood anemones and wood sorrel, while later in the year meadowsweet and honeysuckle scent the air. Keep straight on to **Boon Crag Farm**, joining the road through the National Trust wood yard, where fence posts and other items used by the Trust are made.

Turn left past Monk Coniston, which is now a Holiday Fellowship Guest House and fork left again in 200 yards at the one way road and take the footpath signed 'Tarn Hows'. The track climbs through the wood to the left

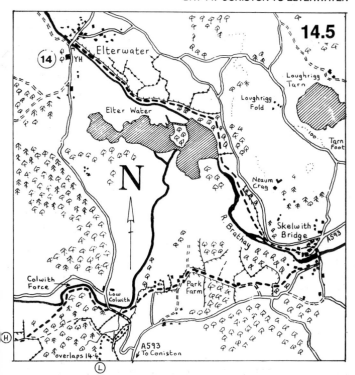

of the stream and then crossing it continues uphill. Taking the second turning left in a third of a mile, the track hairpins back across the stream and then after a similar distance arrives at a tarmac road by a large National Trust car park.

Cross the road and join the throng to stroll down to **Tarn Hows** and round the left side of the lake. The landscaped tarn was originally formed from two or three smaller ones which were dammed to provide water for a sawmill. Keep on the main path which climbs gradually through the trees before descending near the end of the tarn to a T-junction where you turn left and out to an unsurfaced lane. Go left and in half a mile the tarmac road from High Arnside Farm is joined. Descend to cross the main road and turn right taking the permissive footpath through a little wood and then beside the wall through the fields. Crossing a lane, avoid the road to Skelwith Bridge by taking the footpath through **Tongue Intake Plantation** which belongs to the National Trust. After descending to the edge of the wood at a field corner, turn

213

right and over a footbridge to join a little lane which leads out to the main road. Elterwater village and its youth hostel is only just over a mile along the road, but we are going a somewhat circuitous route to sample the delights of the Langdale valley. Turn left for 100 yards and then right over a stile into the fields just before the river, signed 'Skelwith Bridge'.

JOINT ROUTE

Clusters of wood anemones, primroses and celandines grow beside the path which then climbs up through a wood. Crossing a field to pass a solitary house another field brings you to Park Farm which has a slate plaque of the alphabet on its nineteenth-century barn. The track continues through meadows past a cottage, then at the bend take the path across to the wood. Descend through the trees to some houses and the main road where you turn left down to **Skelwith Bridge**.

Crossing the River Brathay turn up to the Kirkstone Galleries and through the yard of the Kirkstone Green Slate Quarries. This was originally a seventeenth-century corn-mill and its water-wheel was fed from the top of the nearby falls. Later it became a bobbin mill, producing bobbins for the cotton industry and the present building, which has circular pillars at the front, was an open drying shed for the wood. Piles of cut slate stand beside the path and a few yards further is Skelwith Force, a fine waterfall. The path now follows the river up Langdale through the fields to the end of Elter Water with the familiar shape of the Langdale Pikes ahead. After passing through a bluebell wood the permissive path kinks left to follow the swiftly flowing river to the village of **Elterwater**.

ELTERWATER

Elterwater is an attractive small village situated a little way beyond the lake of the same name, beside Great Langdale Beck and on the edge of National Trust open common land. The name means 'Swan Lake' and in winter Scandinavian whooper swans sometimes visit Elter Water, where the waters of Great Langdale Beck merge with those of the River Brathay in one of the smallest lakes in the Lake District.

Next to the Britannia Inn, in the centre of the village green, is a large maple tree surrounded by a hexagonal seat. Opposite there is a small shop and for once the youth hostel is close by, only just over the bridge.

But Elterwater has not always been a quiet and unspoilt rural backwater. Just upstream beside Great Langdale Beck was a gunpowder works and from 1824 until around 1918 a large number of people was employed here. The site was chosen because alder tree charcoal was available locally and also, of course, for the water power. The raw materials of saltpetre and sulphur were imported and were initially brought up Windermere to a pier at Brathay though later Windermere station was used. Six water-wheels powered twelve mills and the powders were finely ground before being mixed with powdered charcoal and compressed into slabs using a hydraulic ram. The slabs were then broken up to give particles of the required size which were mixed with graphite and dried, then the gunpowder was put in cartridges and packed into boxes. The whole process was a highly hazardous undertaking and there were many serious accidents. When the works closed, many of the buildings were destroyed in order that no trace of the gunpowder might accidently remain, but a few of the "safe" buildings are left and these have been incorporated into the Langdale Timeshare complex which now occupies the site. The visitors who stay in this luxurious accommodation make a strange contrast to the hard-working employees of earlier years. As one of the former workmen remarked: "Fancy people coming here for their holidays!"

Wood Anemones

The Langdale Pikes from Elterwater

| HIGH LEVEL ROUTE | Distance 11 miles | Ascent 2,900ft |
| LOW LEVEL ROUTE | Distance 6 miles | Ascent 1,400ft |

ROUTE SUMMARY

Both routes stay by Great Langdale Beck to Chapel Stile and then climb steeply to the ridge which leads to the Langdale Pikes.

High Level Route After meandering along the ridge high above Great Langdale the route dips to Stickle Tarn. A stony ascent to Pavey Ark and a bouldery crossing of the Langdale Pikes is followed by the grassy slopes of High Raise. The descent to Easedale Tarn is at first rough, then a good path beside Sourmilk Gill leads down to Easedale and on into Grasmere.

Low Level Route After following the ridge a short cut leads to Easedale Tarn where the routes join down into Easedale.

NOTE: Grasmere may be reached quickly by crossing straight over the ridge.

Although Harrison Stickle, the highest of the Langdale Pikes, reaches only 2,415 feet, much lower than the fells at the head of the valley, the characteristic outline of the Pikes attracts the eye, appearing to dominate the surrounding summits. The rough, craggy shape of these fells, carved and sculpted by the glacier which once flowed down Great Langdale, identifies Harrison Stickle and the precipice of Pavey Ark with the thimble shape of Pike o'Stickle adding the final confirmation. The sight of the Langdale Pikes as we turn off the motorway and head towards the fells always makes us feel that entering the Lake District is coming home.

The approach from Elterwater along the ridge which divides Easedale from Langdale is a quieter way than the usual one up Stickle Ghyll, but after three miles of easy grassy walking it brings you to the same place, where Stickle Tarn lies under the steep cliffs of Pavey Ark. This is one of Lakeland's bigger cliffs, a full 500 feet from the screes at its foot to the bare rocks of its summit, and slanting across the huge face from bottom right to top left is Jack's Rake, a narrow cleft which provides the one weakness that may be attempted by walkers. The usual way, though, is around and up the back, where Pavey Ark is seen to rise by only just enough to justify its status as a separate mountain, being little more than a craggy edge of the main fell, but it would be unthinkable to leave out this top whose summit rocks are worn smooth by the attentions of visitors.

It was a large party that assembled one hot August morning on the screes at the foot of the cliffs. Our family of four had been joined by friends

217

and their two daughters and all were, more or less, looking forward to the climb. Wainwright speaks of it with a mixture of awe and pleasure at having reached the top safely, but the rocks were dry, there was no wind, it was the perfect day. Ahead the rake rose steeply, a narrow scree shoot except that it was almost too steep for scree. As we hesitated and decided on the order of our going, two men, a small boy and a large dog rushed past, hauled themselves up the gangway and disappeared from sight. We looked at each other. "If a dog can do it, so can we," was the general agreement.

The first part although steep has a handrail, a comforting, protecting parapet of rock that holds the drop at bay and soon we were strung out in a long procession. All went well until about three quarters of the way up the cliff; a few mutters of concern, but everyone was enjoying themselves. We then reached the difficult bit; the crux, the exposed move, as the rock climbers put it. The holds were good, the rock was clean, but the protecting parapet was no longer there and below was space. The party stopped, spread out in a long line. Of the small boy and the dog there was no sign. There was a silence. Then at the back of the party a rope was produced from the depths of a rucksack. A leader was appointed and tied to one end while the deputy leader belayed himself to a handy spike of rock. Stepping carefully up onto the sloping ledge, reassuring handholds materialised and he was across. One by one the others followed, encouraged by the advice of seven helpful companions and soon the reassembled party was basking on the summit rocks. This, it was voted afterwards, was the high spot of the holiday.

Our usual way is round the back, up the rocky path that outflanks the cliffs. "You do this for fun?" The teenage girl was surprised to find someone not under the compulsion of teachers and school sweating up the path, but it isn't far and soon the undulating top of the Pikes is reached. You can wander around the tops for hours, though on our last visit in thick mist with twenty-yard visibility most of the wanderers seemed to be lost.

High Raise, little more than a mile distant across the grassy fellside, is aloof, with the Pikes but not of them. A few feet higher than Harrison Stickle, it is generally regarded as being the most central of the Lake District fells and with a distant skyline of hills in all directions it is an excellent viewpoint. As we pitched our mountain tent beside the cairn, to the north were the grey shapes of Skiddaw and Blencathra and to the south Coniston Old Man, but from the doorway of the tent we looked westwards to the sunset and the blue-grey silhouettes of Great Gable and the Scafells. The light faded, the stars came out and above, in the night sky, a shooting star burnt its brief moment of glory.

The descent to Grasmere takes you down to Easedale Tarn, then on past the third and last Sourmilk Gill into Easedale. We are now re-entering Wordsworth territory, but little has been said so far about his devoted younger sister Dorothy. The Wordsworths were a closely knit family and after

William had been left a legacy the two were able to set up house together in Grasmere. Dorothy, in fact, inspired much of William's poetry and while they lived at Grasmere she kept a diary which chronicles the rural life around her. After William's marriage Dorothy continued to live with them, helping with the family chores and with bringing up their children. Sadly she became ill for the last twenty years of her life with what was probably a form of senile dementia and was cared for lovingly by William and his wife until her death in 1855.

The *Journal* is a superb example of Dorothy's work and there can be no more fitting conclusion for this book than to quote what one of England's most gifted and natural writers wrote on December 9th 1801, Wednesday, when she visited Churn Milk Force (Sourmilk Gill) after a very wet spell of weather.

The river came galloping past the Church, as fast as it could come; and when we got into Easedale we saw Churn Milk Force, like a broad stream of snow. At the little footbridge we stopped to look at the company of rivers, which came hurrying down the vale this way and that; it was a valley of streams and islands, with that great waterfall at the head, and lesser falls in different parts of the mountains, coming down to these rivers. We could hear the sound of those lesser falls, but we could not see them. We walked backwards and forwards till all distant objects, except the white shape of the waterfall and the lines of the mountains, were gone. We had the crescent moon when we went out, and at our return there were a few stars that shone dimly, but it was a grey cloudy night.

ROUTE DESCRIPTION

JOINT ROUTE

Taking the minor road from **Elterwater** beside Great Langdale Beck, walk upstream towards Chapel Stile. On the opposite bank is the Langdale Timeshare complex on the site of the old gunpowder works, which blends in discreetly with the surroundings. After about quarter of a mile leave the road for a footpath beside the beck, then crossing the footbridge by the Wainwrights Inn, turn left into **Chapel Stile**. This was built for the quarrymen, but the quarry, which is still being worked, does not intrude upon the houses. At the shop in 200 yards, go right uphill to the Victorian church which was constructed in 1857 replacing an earlier chapel, then go right again and past a row of houses. At the end of the open ground, by the garden wall of a new house, a path leads uphill climbing very steeply and the valley is soon left behind. Below in the ravine is Megs Gill and as the little trod continues climbing, it crosses the gill high up to gain the ridge by a large cairn at a six-way junction.

A short cut may be made to **Grasmere** by going straight across on a good

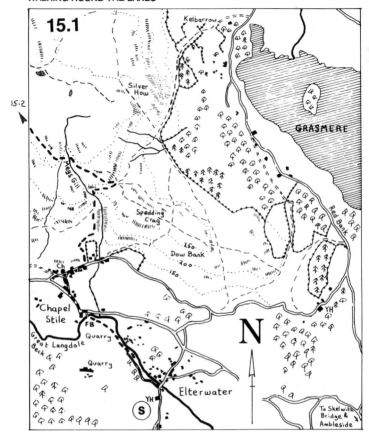

path which descends to follow the wall down to the road by the end of the lake, where you turn left for the village.

From the cairn take the first path to the left which takes a hairpin bend back to recross Megs Gill. Across the valley are the slate quarries, surprisingly close to, but hidden from the village of Chapel Stile and as you emerge from the confines of the ravine, suddenly the mountains appear. Straight ahead the Langdale Pikes look almost alpine, to the left is Bow Fell and the serrated skyline of Crinkle Crags, and rising above the foreground of Lingmoor Fell is Pike o'Blisco. The main path continues to climb along the ridge which

220

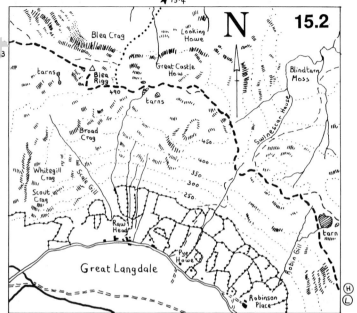

divides Langdale from Easedale and after a very reedy tarn, it joins forces with another path from Silver How. In May the tarn is the nesting place of dozens of black-headed gulls (*Larus ridibundus*). This very gregarious bird breeds in large gulleries and the flocks going to roost often fly in formation.

The route meanders along the ridge and after a mile a group of three small tarns is reached beyond **Great Castle How**. Skirting to the left of the next rocky outcrop and just after passing a perched boulder, a line of cairns heads off to the right down into the valley. This is the start of the Low Level Route to Easedale Tarn, which is now in view from the ridge.

HIGH LEVEL ROUTE

Staying on the ridge the path then climbs past a shelter built under a large boulder to the summit of **Blea Rigg**. Hardly a summit though, a mere bump on the ridge with negligible ascent yet every year it receives innumerable visitors simply because Wainwright made it one of his 214 Lakeland fells. A quarter of a mile beyond the path becomes quite indistinct and veers left in a peaty area leaving the ridge to head straight for Pavey Ark whose 500-foot face rises above **Stickle Tarn**. The 1838 dam enlarging the tarn to supplement

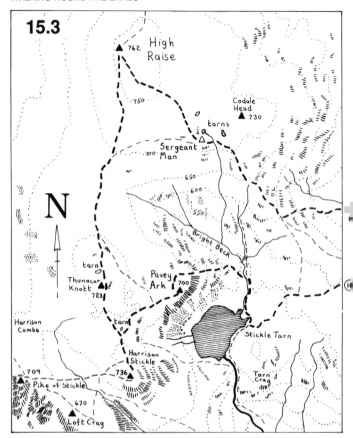

15.3

High Raise ▲ 762

750

Codale Head ▲ 730

tarns

Sergeant Man

700

650

600

550

Bright Beck

N

tarn

Thunacar Knott ▲ 723

Pavey Ark ▲ 700

Harrison Combe

tarn

Stickle Tarn

Harrison Stickle

▲ 709
Pike of Stickle

▲ 736

Tarn Crag

670

▲ Loft Crag

the water supply of the gunpowder works at Elterwater, was restored by the National Park authority in 1959. The line of Jack's Rake can be seen slanting upwards and the doll-like figures of climbers are dwarfed by the massive cliff. The last part of the descent to the tarn may be avoided by short-cutting across the grass to join the Pavey Ark path where it crosses Bright Beck. This broad stony path outflanks the cliffs and after a pleasant scramble of about 600 feet, it emerges into the open a short way from the summit which is on the far side of a section of wall built to deter sheep from suicidal forays. Although the back view of **Pavey Ark** is rather a let-down compared with its

222

Harrison Stickle and Stickle Tarn

tremendous eastern face, it has a fine summit of bare rock and almost beneath your feet far below lies Stickle Tarn. Though many fells are in sight and to the south-east is the large expanse of Windermere, the most impressive feature is the steep but broken rock buttresses of Harrison Stickle.

Several interlinking paths meander westwards across to Harrison Stickle over volcanic rocks and boulders, some rough and coarse with embedded pebbles and others smooth and veined in layers. **Harrison Stickle** is soon reached and from the cairn on its flat rocky top you look westward to Gable and the Scafells or steeply down to the little fields of Langdale. Half a mile to the west, Pike o'Stickle makes an extra top for strong walkers, but most will be happy to save it for another visit and turn back, as there is still a fair way to go. After retracing your steps for a short distance towards Pavey Ark, bear just west of north towards **Thunacar Knott** over grassy slopes for half a mile to where a cairn on the first rocky outcrop marks the top.

223

Camp on High Raise

Passing to the right of a small tarn the path heads towards the highest point in the Central Fells. After dipping to a high col it is an easy half-mile on the broad stony path to **High Raise**. A trig point stands by a huge hollowed-out cairn and this scattering of stones, also known as High White Stones, is generally considered to be the most central fell of the Lake District. Although as a summit it is rather ordinary, an extensive upland sheep pasture without precipices or rocky edges, as a viewpoint it is excellent and in whichever direction you look the view is all of mountains. This is the penultimate top of the walk and in clear weather nearly all the mountains visited in the last two weeks can be seen. Beyond the Langdale Pikes lie Crinkle Crags and Bow Fell and further still are the Coniston fells. To the west lie the Scafells and high above the head of Langstrath rises the huge bulk of Great Gable. Grasmoor and the North-Western Fells are only ten miles away, but more than a week has passed since they were explored. To the north are Skiddaw and Blencathra, eastward is the full length of the Helvellyn range, while on the far distant skyline, just peeping above the Fairfield Horseshoe, are High Street and the Kentmere fells.

The final top is just out of sight but, heading south-east on an improving

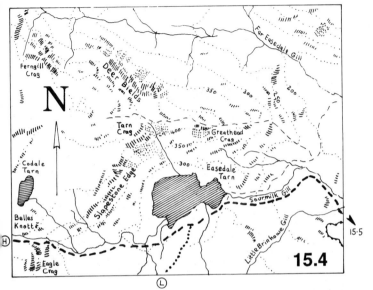

path join a line of fence posts, then just before a little tarn turn away to the rocky crest of **Sergeant Man**. Although with an insignificant ascent it does not rank as a separate mountain, this little bump has a very distinctive shape and is surprisingly easy to identify on the skyline in many distant views. The top has a small cairn which looks across Bright Beck to Pavey Ark. A good path descends to cross a little gill where, beyond a marshy area is Codale Head, not very often visited but quite definitely a separate 2,000-foot summit. Stickle Tarn now comes into view on the right and after passing a large, flat rock slab, Easedale Tarn appears to the left. The path picks its way down through rocky outcrops to a flattish col where, well cairned, it turns off left downhill. A less obvious path continues along the ridge to Blea Rigg.

Easedale Tarn is straight ahead and to the left Codale Tarn lies sheltered in its grassy bowl. It is a good mile to **Easedale Tarn**, descending steeply beside a pretty little gill on a rocky path. To the right are Eagle Crag and Blea Crag on the northern flank of Blea Rigg.

LOW LEVEL ROUTE
This is really a short cut which avoids the high ground and extra miles of the High Level Route. After an initially steep descent to the east of Blea Crag, the little path slants right at an easy angle to rejoin the returning High Level Route about half way along **Easedale Tarn**.

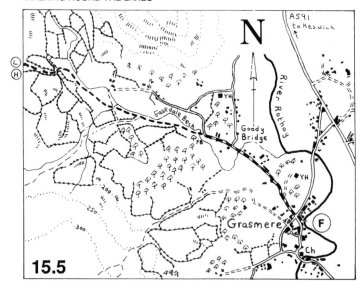

JOINT ROUTE

Becoming easier underfoot the path skirts **Easedale Tarn**, a beautiful expanse of water. Old guidebooks speak of the refreshment hut which once stood by the tarn, but this was in ruins by the early 1960s and a few stones by a boulder near the outflow are all that remain. Descending by the stream, ahead is Helm Crag, with its summit rocks silhouetted against the sky then pastoral **Easedale** soon comes into view and the path continues down to the valley beside the cascades and waterfalls of Sourmilk Gill. After a couple of gates the path continues beside Easedale Beck through daisy-sprinkled fields for another half mile to a footbridge by a ford in a little wood. Turn right on Easedale Road and it is now about half a mile to the centre of **Grasmere** and the end of the walk.

GRASMERE

If you didn't have time to look round Grasmere at the beginning of the walk now is the time to buy your souvenirs. One of the disadvantages of backpacking is that all tempting purchases, unless they are small and light or are to be consumed pretty soon, must be left for another visit.

Souvenirs are about all you will be able to buy in Grasmere. If you want a woolly jumper or a bottle of perfume, a fizzy drink or a piece of gingerbread then Grasmere rules OK, but the only shop to sell food closes early. It is all part of a cunning scheme to get you to eat out in Grasmere and the same applies to campsites. There aren't any. Fortunately though Grasmere has not one, but two youth hostels. Thorney How, an old Lakeland farmhouse, is a mile out of the village on the Easedale side and Butharlyp How is a Lakeland-stone Victorian house with a beautiful garden, particularly in rhododrendron time. There is also the Heaton Cooper Studio and an excellent bookshop. Rowing boats may be hired on the lake and buses taken to Keswick or Windermere.

Of course, Grasmere has not always been a tourist mecca. Built on the old packhorse route to Whitehaven, which was turnpiked in 1761, most of the houses date from the ninteenth century. The old road led past Dove Cottage and the main road beside the lake was blasted out in 1830. In the sixteenth century there were eighteen fulling mills here, probably similar to the number of gift shops today.

Many of the visitors come to see Wordsworth's grave in the churchyard of Saint Oswald. Until the fourteenth century the dead were taken the sixteen miles to Kendal for burial, but the Black Death in 1348 and the need for a local graveyard led to the consecration of the medieval chapel in Grasmere the following year. There is an annual rushbearing ceremony on August 5 which has taken place since the sixteenth century when fresh rushes were gathered and put in the church to replace the old ones covering the cold, bare earth floor. The custom continued here because the church remained unflagged until 1840. Another festivity is Grasmere Sports which is held on the Thursday nearest to August 20 each year. Hound trails, the guides fell race, Cumberland wrestling and all the other more usual fête activities give an entertaining day in this, one of the most popular of Lakeland's villages.

CONCLUSION

For the walkers who didn't start their walk at Grasmere, tomorrow is another day's holiday with the delights of Fairfield or Rydal to look forward to. But for many this is it, finis, the end. Some will be returning again in a few weeks or months but others will not be back again for a year or even longer.

However, if on arriving in Grasmere you don't want your holiday to finish, you can always go round again. It's not like the Pennine Way where you end up 250 miles from where you started. Here the end is also the beginning, and with two routes to choose from each day there are, for the mathematically inclined, exactly 32,768 different ways of doing the walk!

And why not explore further afield, look around the corner, try another way up. The Lake District is endless and you could walk every day for the rest of your life and still not see all its hidden corners, secret pathways and quiet places.

Jeremy on Helm Crag

THE LINK ROSTHWAITE TO GRASMERE

HIGH LEVEL ROUTE	Distance 8 miles	Ascent 2,150ft
LOW LEVEL ROUTE	Distance 7¹/₂ miles	Ascent 1,700ft

ROUTE SUMMARY

The way to Grasmere lies over Greenup Edge and for the first four miles there is no choice about the route which leads through the village of Stonethwaite and then climbs steeply beside Greenup Gill to cross Greenup Edge into the head of Far Easedale.

High Level Route Although actually lower than Greenup Edge, this pleasant ridge leads over Calf Crag and Gibson Knott to Helm Crag before dropping to Grasmere.

Low Level Route The sheltered and secluded valley of Far Easedale leads down gently to Grasmere.

Greenup Edge is hardly an edge at all, just a green, grassy and rather boggy high level pass in the Central Fells midway between High Raise, the most central fell in the Lake District, and Ullscarf, perhaps one of the wettest. But if the pass itself lacks interest, the approaches on either side have more to offer. As you leave Rosthwaite the hamlet of Stonethwaite is approached by a narrow road past the new school. Close by is the parish church of Saint Andrew which was consecrated in 1687 and then the road comes to an end amid a cluster of cottages and farm buildings. Like Rosthwaite and Seathwaite, Stonethwaite was a Norse settlement, thwaite meaning clearing, and from 1195 it belonged to the monks of Fountains Abbey in Yorkshire.

In the churchyard is the grave of Bob Graham and it was his record run of 42 peaks and 32,000 feet of ascent in 23 hours that inspired one of our earliest backpacks in the Lakes. There are also other connections with fell running at Stonethwaite as the local runner Chris Bland was the first to attempt all the Wainwrights in a week; that is one volume a day for seven days, climbing in turn all the fells in each book. Every day was planned to start and finish at one of the parish churches as the run was organised to raise money for the Borrowdale church roof. On five days he succeeded, an incredible achievement and here the record stands for although Jos Naylor has since linked all the 214 summits in a continuous run over seven days, the fells were taken in the most convenient order and did not fit the perfection of one book a day.

At the road end stands the Langstrath Hotel where we have stayed on several occasions. Ian, who was then the landlord is a fell runner, too, and helped Chris Bland on his record run. After serving lunch for his guests Ian

WALKING ROUND THE LAKES

takes off into the hills for a couple of hours running before returning to prepare the next meal. John was once invited to join one of these training runs which started with a direct ascent of Rosthwaite Fell, continued over Glaramara and Allen Crags to Esk Hause, and returned via Ruddy Gill and Seathwaite. After some eleven miles and 2,500 feet of climbing in two hours John collapsed exhausted at the hotel while Ian went back to work to cook thirty dinners.

It may seem strange to those who have always drunk from Lakeland mountain streams, but until the day of that run we used to carry our drinking water up into the hills. Our education came later that evening when Ian popped his head round the door asking: "Fancy another run?" We were ready for a bath, but the water had been off for some time, not unusual before dinner with heavy demands being made on an inadequate pipe network, but even approaching bedtime the supply was still not restored. Fellow guests were beginning to mutter. In answer to our surprised look Ian explained he was going to fix the water supply. Setting off up the hillside and after ten minutes' climb, a large tank appeared. "As I thought", said Ian, "the pipe's broken." It led straight out of the stream into the tank. This was the wholesome 'tap water' we had been carrying back up onto the fells! The pipe was quickly fixed and since then we have always used the natural supplies on the hills.

There is plenty of it on the slopes above Stonethwaite and cascading down Greenup Gill to join Langstrath Beck at Smithymire Island. In medieval times this was the site of an iron smelter and iron ore was brought here by packhorse train all the way from Ore Gap on the slopes of Bow Fell above Great Langdale. Although Stonethwaite belonged to Fountains Abbey, Borrowdale was at this time in the hands of Furness Abbey and towards the end of the fourteenth century the two abbeys were in dispute about the ownership of Stonethwaite which the Furness monks claimed was rightly theirs.

Perhaps the wettest place of all is just off the route at the head of the Wythburn valley where the map records the place simply as 'The Bog'. There are no such problems, though, with the route choices beyond, either following Far Easedale gently down beside the gill or traversing the pleasant ridge which culminates in Helm Crag overlooking Grasmere and the end of the journey.

There will be plenty of company on the Link as this is the way followed by Wainwright's Coast to Coast travellers, which since the television series has become very popular. But these walkers are rushing things, hurrying through the Lake District intent upon their long journey to the east coast, whereas we have spent a week enjoying the mountains and valleys, villages and towns, tarns and lakes, and have yet another week still to come.

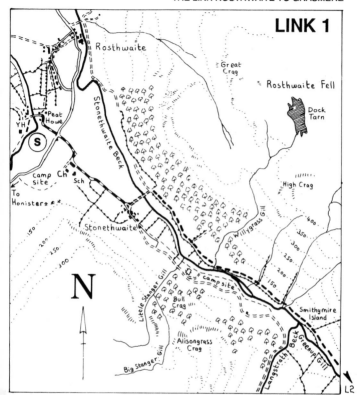

ROUTE DESCRIPTION

From Longthwaite Youth Hostel at **Rosthwaite** cross the bridge to Peat Howe, go up the lane and then straight across the road towards **Stonethwaite**, past the new school and the council houses, which were built on the site of the old school of 1825.

By the phone box in the tiny hamlet, a bridleway signed 'Greenup Edge' goes down to Stonethwaite Bridge which was rebuilt in 1979 replacing an earlier bridge of 1899. Like Seathwaite on the far side of Rosthwaite Fell this valley was badly flooded in August 1966 with the water over 10 feet deep.

After crossing the beck follow it upstream towards Eagle Crag for nearly a mile to the confluence of Langstrath Beck and Greenup Gill. Don't cross the

231

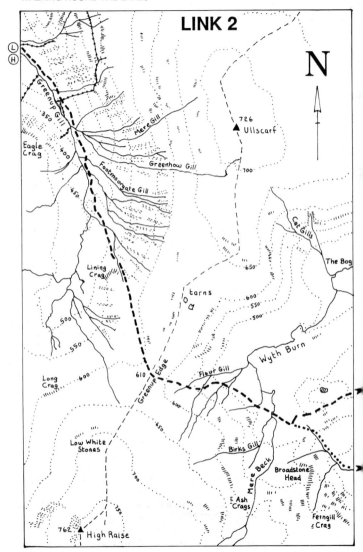

LINK 2

N

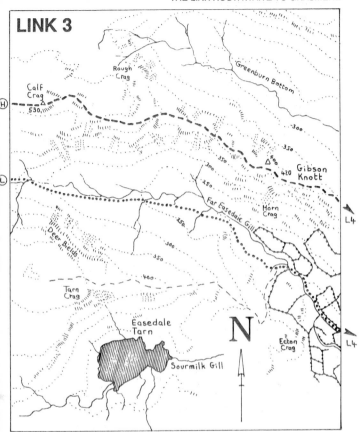

footbridge, which was erected in memory of Gordon Hallworth who unable to cross the flooded beck died of exhaustion in the dale in 1939, but follow Greenup Gill past Smithymire Island where Fountains Abbey had its iron smelter. The path gradually climbs beside the gill with its little falls and on the right are the cliffs of Eagle Crag. After a mile there is a short respite as the angle eases and the path leaves the stream in an area of moraines, but then the ascent starts again much steeper, up beside Lining Crag with the goal, the summit of the pass, still out of sight above. It is a good 400ft before the angle again relents at the top of the crag from which there are birds-eye views

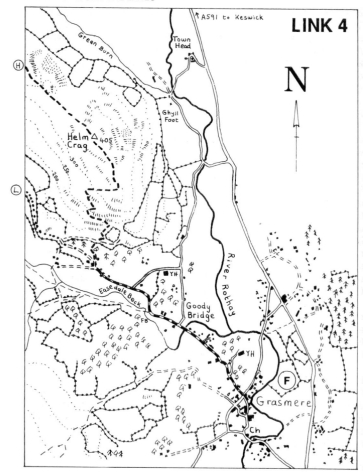

of the moraines and the meandering beck, then as the path disappears into a boggy section, **Greenup Edge** is reached. It hardly feels like an edge, a broad grassy moorlike col with bog stretching away on either hand, but a line of cairns marks the way across and at the far side the view down into Wythburn appears.

Straight ahead is a dip in the skyline where the path crosses into Far

234

Easedale, but the head of the Wythburn valley, which drops towards Thirlmere, must first be traversed to reach the col. This is rather boggy and as fast as a path develops it is avoided by people trying to keep their feet dry. A metal ladder stile crosses the long vanished fence at the head of **Far Easedale** where the High and Low Level Routes divide. On the northern side of the valley is the ridge which terminates in Helm Crag, while ahead Far Easedale Gill leads gently down to Grasmere.

HIGH LEVEL ROUTE

The path along the ridge follows the edge to **Calf Crag** whose top has a small cairn from which the ridge stretches on to Helm Crag with Grasmere beyond while to the left lies the mass of the Helvellyn range and Fairfield. Then it is an easy amble along the ridge to **Gibson Knott** in another mile where the little cairn looks down on the lower reaches of Far Easedale and across to Easedale Tarn with the Langdale Pikes on the skyline beyond. From here it is a gentle descent to the col before Helm Crag and a short but steep ascent to the final top on the ridge. **Helm Crag** has the best summit, it is, in fact, one of the best summits on the walk and is also the most difficult to reach despite its lowly status, with an entertaining scramble to the very top of the rocks. The rock outcrops at the northern end of the ridge give the fell its other name of the Lion and the Lamb while those at the southern end resemble an old woman playing the organ when seen from below and give fine views of Grasmere and over to Sourmilk Gill.

A good path, worn by the thousands for whom Helm Crag is the only objective, sets off down the ridge towards Grasmere before swinging right to avoid an eroded section. The recently repaired path then zigzags down the fellside into **Easedale** finally turning left at the track junction to join the tarmac lane which leads down into **Grasmere** in just over half a mile.

LOW LEVEL ROUTE

Descending into **Far Easedale** the gill is followed down into the valley with an attractive cascade before the stone walls of the valley fields are reached. A rough track brings you to **Easedale** where the High Level Route comes down from Helm Crag and the road is joined at Goody Bridge for the final half mile to **Grasmere**.

CONCLUSION

Back in Grasmere after a week exploring the Eastern and Northern Fells, the Western and Southern Fells still beckon. The giants of Lakeland, Gable and Pillar, the Scafells, Bow Fell and the Crinkles, the gentler Coniston fells and the valleys, Wasdale, Eskdale and Great Langdale, the villages of Boot, Coniston and Elterwater. Miles of some of the best fell walking in Cumbria. Who can resist? You will be back, won't you?

GENERAL INFORMATION

This table can only be taken as a guide as although up to date in 1991, things are always changing.

DAY	PLACE	YHA	PUB/ HOTEL	B&B	CAMP SITE	SHOP PO	TEL	WC	BUS	OTHER
	GRASMERE	✓✓	✓	✓	-	FGP	✓	✓	✓	? Dove Cottage
	Rydal	-	✓	✓	-	-	✓	-	✓	Rydal Mount
	Ambleside	✓	✓	✓	-	FPG	✓	✓	✓M	? cinema
1	TROUTBECK	✓	✓	✓	✓	FP	✓	-	M	Town End
	Hartsop	-	1m	✓	1m	-	✓	-	M	
2	PATTERDALE	✓	✓	✓	✓	FP	✓	✓	✓M	
3	GLENRIDDING	✓	✓	✓	✓	FPG	✓	✓	✓M	? steamers
	Stanah	✓	½m	✓	½m	-	✓	-	✓	
4	THRELKELD	4m	NA	✓	✓	FP	✓	-	✓	
5	KESWICK	✓	✓	✓	✓	FPG	✓	✓	✓M	? boats 2 museums cinema, theatre
	Braithwaite	-	✓	✓	✓	FP	✓	✓	✓	
6	BUTTERMERE	✓	✓	✓	✓	-	✓	✓	M	
7	HONISTER	✓	-	-	-	-	-	-	-	
	Seatoller	-	-	✓	✓	-	✓	✓	✓	?
	Grange	-	✓	✓	✓	-	✓	✓	✓	
8	ROSTHWAITE	✓	✓	✓	✓	PF	✓	✓	✓	
9	BLACK SAIL	✓	-	-	-	-	-	-	-	
10	WASDALE HEAD	4m	✓	✓	✓	Gf	✓	✓	-	
11	BOOT	✓	✓	✓	✓	Pf	✓	-	-	railway water mill
12	GREAT LANGDALE	4m	✓	✓	✓	-	✓	-	✓	
13	CONISTON	✓✓	✓	✓	✓	FPG	✓	✓	✓	? boats museum gallery
	Skelwith Br	-	✓	✓	-	-	✓	-	✓	
14	ELTERWATER	✓	✓	✓	✓	F	✓	✓	✓	
	Chapel Stile	-	✓	✓	✓	PF	✓	✓	✓	

Key

✔	facility available
-	facility not available
$\frac{1}{2}$m	distance in miles to nearest YHA/hotel/campsite
F	shop selling food
f	shop selling a small amount of food only
P	Post Office
G	shop selling outdoor gear
NA	pub does meals, but no accommodation
M	Mountain goat bus service
?	Information Centre

Youth Hostels

Some hostels are shut for one or more nights each week while some are only open in the summer, also over the years hostels close and new ones are opened. At the time of writing the book, starting from Grasmere on Saturday in the summer months coincided with open nights all the way round, but it is advisable to check with the current YHA Accomodation Guide when planning the walk. If there is no hostel the distance to the nearest is given in miles. For an up-to-date list of YHA Accommodation contact:

YHA, Trevelyan House, 8 St Stephen's Hill, St Albans, Herts AL1 2DY. Tel (0727) 55215

Hotels, Pubs, B&B

Accommodation information can be obtained by contacting the nearest tourist information centre. Each centre is responsible for its own local area, but for a list of addresses and telephone numbers contact:

Windermere Tourist Information Centre, Victoria Street, Windermere, Cumbria. Tel 05394 64699.

Campsites

Apart from Grasmere, the Lake District is well supplied with campsites. Details can be obtained from the information centres as above.

Post Offices and Shops

Many of the villages have a post office which also sells food, but it may close early or not open on some days, so it is advisable to check beforehand if you are relying on it. The other shops sell food and sometimes walking gear.

Buses

Bus services are less frequent during the winter and often don't run at all on Sundays. The Mountain Goat service operates only in the summer. Further information may be obtained from the information centres above.

DISTANCES AND ASCENTS

DAY	ROUTE	HIGH LEVEL		LOW LEVEL	
		distance	ascent	distance	ascent
1.	Grasmere to Troutbeck	12 ½m	3,700ft	8m	1,200ft
2.	Troutbeck to Patterdale	13m	3,550ft	11m	1,750ft
3.	Patterdale to Glenridding	6 ½m	3,050ft	4m	1000ft
4.	Glenridding to Threlkeld	8 ½m	2,500ft	8 ½m	1,800ft
5.	Threlkeld to Keswick	12m	4,350ft	8m	950ft
6.	Keswick to Buttermere	12m	3,800ft	10m	1,250ft
7.	Buttermere to Honister	7m	3,450ft	5 ½m	1,450ft
8.	Honister to Rosthwaite	10m	2,100ft	6 ½m	350ft
9.	Rosthwaite to Black Sail	6m	2,750ft	6m	2,050ft
10.	Black Sail to Wasdale Head	9m	3,300ft	3m	900ft
11.	Wasdale Head to Eskdale	9m	4,000ft	7 ½m	750ft
12.	Eskdale to Great Langdale	11m	3,500ft	8m	2,100ft
13.	Langdale to Coniston	8 ½m	4,000ft	7m	1,600ft
14.	Coniston to Elterwater	9m	2,050ft	9m	850ft
15.	Elterwater to Grasmere	11m	2,900ft	6m	1,400ft
TOTAL		**145m**	**49,000ft**	**108m**	**19,000ft**
Link.	Rosthwaite to Grasmere	8m	2150ft	7 ½m	1700ft

CICERONE GUIDES

Cicerone publish a wide range of reliable guides to walking and climbing in Britain - and other general interest books

LAKE DISTRICT - General Books
LAKELAND VILLAGES
WORDSWORTH'S DUDDON REVISITED
THE REGATTA MEN
REFLECTIONS ON THE LAKES
OUR CUMBRIA
PETTIE
THE HIGH FELLS OF LAKELAND
CONISTON COPPER A History
LAKELAND - A taste to remember (Recipes)
THE LOST RESORT?
CHRONICLES OF MILNTHORPE
LOST LANCASHIRE

LAKE DISTRICT - Guide Books
CASTLES IN CUMBRIA
WESTMORLAND HERITAGE WALK
IN SEARCH OF WESTMORLAND
CONISTON COPPER MINES
SCRAMBLES IN THE LAKE DISTRICT
MORE SCRAMBLES IN THE LAKE DISTRICT
WINTER CLIMBS IN THE LAKE DISTRICT
WALKS IN SILVERDALE/ARNSIDE
BIRDS OF MORECAMBE BAY
THE EDEN WAY

NORTHERN ENGLAND (outside the Lakes
THE YORKSHIRE DALES A walker's guide
WALKING IN THE SOUTH PENNINES
LAUGHS ALONG THE PENNINE WAY
WALKS IN THE YORKSHIRE DALES (3 VOL)
WALKS TO YORKSHIRE WATERFALLS
NORTH YORK MOORS Walks
THE CLEVELAND WAY & MISSING LINK
DOUGLAS VALLEY WAY
THE RIBBLE WAY
WALKING NORTHERN RAILWAYS EAST
WALKING NORTHERN RAILWAYS WEST
HERITAGE TRAILS IN NW ENGLAND
BIRDWATCHING ON MERSEYSIDE
THE LANCASTER CANAL
FIELD EXCURSIONS IN NW ENGLAND
ROCK CLIMBS LANCASHIRE & NW
THE ISLE OF MAN COASTAL PATH

DERBYSHIRE & EAST MIDLANDS
WHITE PEAK WALKS - 2 Vols
HIGH PEAK WALKS
WHITE PEAK WAY
KINDER LOG
THE VIKING WAY
THE DEVIL'S MILL (Novel)
WHISTLING CLOUGH (Novel)
WALES & WEST MIDLANDS
THE RIDGES OF SNOWDONIA
HILLWALKING IN SNOWDONIA
ASCENT OF SNOWDON
WELSH WINTER CLIMBS
SNOWDONIA WHITE WATER SEA & SURF
SCRAMBLES IN SNOWDONIA
ROCK CLIMBS IN WEST MIDLANDS
THE SHROPSHIRE HILLS A Walker's Guide
SOUTH & SOUTH WEST ENGLAND
WALKS IN KENT
THE WEALDWAY & VANGUARD WAY
SOUTH DOWNS WAY & DOWNS LINK
COTSWOLD WAY
WALKING ON DARTMOOR
SOUTH WEST WAY - 2 Vol

SCOTLAND
SCRAMBLES IN LOCHABER
SCRAMBLES IN SKYE
THE ISLAND OF RHUM
CAIRNGORMS WINTER CLIMBS
WINTER CLIMBS BEN NEVIS & GLENCOE
SCOTTISH RAILWAY WALKS
TORRIDON A Walker's Guide
SKI TOURING IN SCOTLAND

THE MOUNTAINS OF ENGLAND & WALES
VOL 1 WALES
VOL 2 ENGLAND

Also a full range of guidebooks to walking, scrambling, ice-climbing, rock climbing, and other adventurous pursuits in Europe

---

Other guides are constantly being added to the Cicerone List.
Available from bookshops, outdoor equipment shops or direct (send for price list)
from CICERONE, 2 POLICE SQUARE, MILNTHORPE, CUMBRIA, LA7 7PY